A MOM'S GUIDE
TO SURVIVING HIGH SCHOOL ATHLETICS

D0731722

Other books written by
Michelle Whitaker Winfrey

<u>Children's Books</u>
It's My Birthday ... Finally! A Leap Year Story

It's My Birthday ... Finally – Activity and Workbook

It's Not Leap Year this Year! A Leap Year Story

<u>Religious</u>
Yours, Mine & God's
Giving and Receiving: All for the Love of the God and the Church

A MOM'S GUIDE
TO SURVIVING HIGH SCHOOL ATHLETICS

Michelle Whitaker Winfrey

Hobby House Publishing Group
P.O. Box 1527
Jackson, NJ 08527

hobbyhousepublishinggroup.com

ISBN: 978-0-9727179-7-7

Library of Congress Control Number: 2010909745

Frog carrying mushroom with or without the double H is a Trademark of Hobby House Publishing Group

Printed in the United States of America

This book is dedicated to
my son Miles and his friends who played
sports in high school, especially

Jesse – Football
Anthony – Football
Josh – Football
Kerwin – Football & Track
Justin – Football & Basketball
Tylor – Football & Track
Vinnie - Track

… and their moms for "surviving" with me!

Edited by Jeannette Cézanne
Customline Wordware
customline.com

Acknowledgements
To all the parents of high school student-athletes who assisted me in the research for this book.

A special thanks to Pablo Chavez for suggesting I write this book, and Illysa Weisbrod and Bill Oliver for their many suggestions and countless hours of proofreading.

To Marie Bailey for allowing me to use her as our mom expert and Michael A. Taylor for his do's and don't list for sports parents.

Without the approval from the
National Collegiate Scouting Association (NCSA),
chapter 16 would not exist as it does. I cannot thank them enough for their permission to use their information; to use them as a resource.

Thank you to the following for providing the information in the "Perspective" sections:

Mr. John Lamela, athletic director, and Coach Margaret Harris.

A MOM'S GUIDE
TO SURVIVING HIGH SCHOOL ATHLETICS

Table of Contents

Chapters	Page

A MOM'S GUIDE
TO SURVIVING HIGH SCHOOL ATHLETICS

On your mark, get set...

INTRODUCTION

As the mom of a high school athlete, who walked into this new world without the knowledge of high school athletics—as they're conducted today—I found myself on a fast learning curve during my son's freshman year. In one year, we experienced high school football, bowling, and weight training; the next year track and field was thrown into the mix. My carefully planned schedule was thrown out the window. My budget maneuvered and my grocery bill almost doubled. Thankfully, we had the extra refrigerator in the garage! Although he'd been an athlete since the age of five, somehow high school sports really kick-started my son's metabolism, and he was eating four full meals a day.

What I learned over the past four years as the mom of a high school athlete includes injury management, nutrition and health for the athlete, a balance of academics and sports, and the new world of college recruiting, all of which I am now sharing with you.

Part of this learning curve was who to listen to and who to ignore. Parents who had their first child in high school, because their son or daughter played sports in middle school or since they'd been kids, thought they knew everything there was to know about high school sports. What I quickly discovered is that they knew a lot about Little League and Pop Warner and continued to treat their son or daughter, and the coach, as though they were still in Little League or Pop Warner. However, they didn't know any more than I did about high school sports. Only those who had children who were upperclassmen, or who had children who'd graduated from high school already, really had somewhat of a clue.

On football game day, my son's day began at 6:45 am when he left for school; it ended between 9:30 and 10:30 at night, depending upon whether the game was home or away. He usually had about two hours after school to rest, eat, and start homework. By the end of his freshman year, he figured out a system that allowed him to do his homework between classes, or when class work was complete and there was time to spare. For a child who enjoys taking his time to sit and mull over his homework, and complete it piece by piece with breaks in between for eating this lack of free time caught him by surprise!

Caught me by surprise, too! Bowling was a little easier. He was usually home between 6:30 and 7:00 pm. But he didn't have the opportunity to come home in between for something to eat and start his homework, because bowling was usually right after school. Track turned out to be another sport that required long days, too. The greatest ease came with his junior and senior years when he and many of his friends were driving. Suddenly, we (moms) didn't have to worry about getting our student-athletes to and from school in the middle of the day, and picking them up late after the games were over! Believe me, by the time junior year rolled around, we were all happy about not having to run around so much... however, we now shared a new concern ... teen driving.

I would have loved to attend a parent meeting where the topic of discussion was "what to expect from high school sports." Knowing that my son would be getting home at 10:30 pm and still be expected to have his homework done for the next day would have helped me help him.

This is why I have developed the *Parents' High School Sports Education Group (PHSEd Group)*. Through this organization, middle schools, high schools, parent organizations, and booster clubs invite me to speak with parents about high school sports and what to expect. The lectures can be sport-specific, or focused on the general concerns surrounding high school sports. There are times when a coach is experiencing a problem, such as lack of volunteers, and needs me to come in and explain what can be lost or come out of your pocket if fundraising isn't done. I can also review the expectations set by the coach, and since I too am a mom, the tone of my presentation is more maternal, more intimate, rather than sounding like a coach.

My goal for "*A Mom's Guide for Surviving High School Athletics*" is to give parents, moms in particular, the information they need to help their student-athletes, their children, and families towards having the best four years of high school sports possible.

Mʏ Sᴛᴏʀʏ

After the last game of the season is played,
and all the glory fades from wins past,
it is our educated high school graduates
who are the winners

During his senior year, late on a Friday night, I watched my son during a high school football game collide with two other players and go down ... along with the other players. His teammate stayed down, the opposing teammate they were after jumped up and my son wobbled his way up to his feet. Help ran to the teammate who was down and rightfully so. During the commotion, my son had somehow wandered off to the sidelines. Still wobbling, he paced the area behind his teammates while the game continued, with his neck cocked to one side, helmet off and a strange look on his face.

Turning to the friend beside me, I said, "Look at Miles, doesn't he look strange to you?"

"Oh yeah, I bet he's got a stinger, see how he's holding and rubbing his neck. It looks like a bad one," she said.

A stinger! That would explain it: I knew what that was. Okay, not so bad ... or so I thought. I continued to watch Miles and wondered why he wouldn't tell someone that his neck hurt. He was obviously in pain. Understanding that I should not go down to the field during the game, I stayed in my seat and watched my son.

The offense was in. Good, Miles played defense, so this would give him a rest and the clock was running down. Eleven seconds, ten seconds, nine seconds, and then finally zero. The first half was over. Before they ran off to the locker room, I went down and tried to get his attention—or the attention of the athletic trainer—without any luck, and off they went to the locker room.

When the team came back out, they began to warm up, but Miles was once again pacing behind the line. The athletic trainer, along with another gentleman, walked over to him. The gentleman began making an assessment of his injury. Soon the three of them turned toward the stands and looked up. Who are they looking for? Me! The mom! I went down to the field to speak with the athletic trainer and the other gentleman, who turned out to be an orthopedic doctor. My son was being pulled for the rest of the game and we were given instructions to bring him to the doctor's office the following day. *Must have been more serious than I thought*, I realized.

Tomorrow was Saturday, and they didn't want us to wait until Monday.

I spoke with Miles, who assured me that he was okay, so back to my seat I went to watch the rest of the game and root for his team. What was there left for me to do?

Time to pray!

Nothing else I could do, because my son is now out of the hands of the coach and athletic trainer and in the hands of God. A new game was now being played.

As a marketing professional, my job requires that I travel. And sure enough, I had to be on a plane the next morning at seven o'clock, heading to Dallas, Texas, for the next four days. Giving my husband instructions, I left, knowing that Miles was in good hands. Midday on Saturday, my husband called me. Our son had a concussion, a stinger, neck pain, and weakness in the left arm and shoulder (which we discovered was due in part to multiple stingers over the past weeks). He needed an MRI, an EMG, some x-rays, and to see a spine specialist.

I spoke with the doctor, who further explained that due to the concussion, Miles couldn't play or practice for at least one week, pending the test results. I also spoke with Miles who was not in great pain. Just some discomfort and weakness, and he had a mild headache.

Two days later, while I was still in Dallas, I went to lunch with two friends who were aware of what was happening with my son back at home. We talked about high school sports and the lack of information for parents, about how some coaches have too much authority over our children and how some players play injured—despite the increased risk for themselves and their teammates. We all agreed that while the coach is the coach, the player is our child ... and, ultimately, at the high school level, the parent is—or should be—involved. So there we sat in this wonderful Mexican restaurant in Dallas and *A Mom's Guide to Surviving High School Athletics* was born before lunch was over!

Once I got home, I found myself in a whirlwind of doctors and tests. The diagnosis was quite dismal. "Miles should never participate in any contact sport ever again for the rest of his life," was what the first two specialists told us. (This not only included football, but basketball and in fact any other sport where two players have the possibility of colliding with each other.) Wow! That was a jolt.

My first concern was depression. How would this affect Miles mentally and emotionally? We talked about it. He said he was fine and would just move on to throwing the shot put and disc next season. I could tell that he was sad, but I appreciated that he had the support of his friends and coach.

As his mother, I watched him closely for signs of depression. Thankfully, we didn't have to add this to our list of medical issues!

My second concern had to do with the type and quality of life he would have in the future. With this concern, I called my sister-in-law—an associate dean of nursing—as well as his pediatrician to ask their advice, and they felt strongly that we should have all of the tests reviewed by at least two additional doctors. Which we did.

It took almost two months of doctor visits and physical therapy sessions. The end result was that Miles regained full use and strength of his left arm and shoulder. However, he has multiple neck issues that will be with him for the rest of his life. Although full-contact football is out of the question, he can enjoy intramural sports. He must remain aware of his limitations and work on strengthening his neck muscles. If he experiences any type of neck pain or trauma, back to the doctor we must go.

My son dodged a bullet and a bittersweet high school football career was over.

In the football games he did play that last season as a senior, he played better than ever. He was in the newspaper twice; and as a defensive lineman who stepped into the role of goal line fullback for the first time, he scored a touchdown. Of course I caught it on tape!

He went on to throwing the shot put for the varsity track team in winter and spring, and is getting ready for college in the fall.

Since he was on track to play football in college (there were several college coaches talking with him), we contacted his recruiter and informed him of the news, and asked him to stop all further recruiting efforts. Thankfully, Miles was registered with the National Collegiate Scouting Association, (NCSA), which not only released us from our recruiting contract immediately, but sent us a full refund for all monies paid.

High school athletic careers are what our children make of them. It is what we help them live through. Some come out on top and others have to learn to live through challenges and adversity. Hopefully, they all end up in the same place ... in line to receive their high school diplomas.

I am grateful that I can share all that I have learned and hope that your family's high school athletic experience will be enhanced by this book.

Oh, and remember, Mom ... share this book with your children. Maybe not the entire book, but sections that you feel warrant their attention. Perhaps just leave it on the kitchen table and let them discover it!

Michelle Winfrey,
The High School Sports Mom

Who is involved in high school athletics?

Parent/Family

Athletic Coach

Athletic Trainer

Student-Athlete

Principal

Athletic Director

Teammates

When high school is over, I want my son's life to continue as a healthy young man
Spiritually - Mentally - Physically

LESSONS YOUR CHILD CAN *LIVE* WITH

was developed out of a conversation with good friend, Bill Oliver.

The emphasis here is *LIVE*.

The lessons appear throughout the book.
Look for this icon:

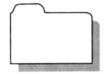

Lesson I – Be committed

Lesson II – Respect others

Lesson III – Who is the mom and who is the coach?

Lesson IV – Be involved

Lesson V – It takes money

Lesson VI – Observe the chain of communication

Lesson VII – Reveal and share symptoms

Lesson VIII – Health and nutrition are vital to success

Lesson IX – Plan ahead

Lesson X – Don't forget to say thanks to those who have

helped along the way

1 – So, Your Child Wants to Play High School Sports!

Get ready for a great time!

Depending upon the size of the school district and town, your child's high school may offer several different sports, of which many are broken down between two divisions: varsity and junior varsity (JV). Some sports, such as football, may also have a third division called freshman.

Don't assume that if your child has never played sports that he or she will not play them in high school, or that the sport they've been playing since they were ten years old will be their chosen sport in high school. Things change; kids change.

My son began bowling when he was four years old. By the time he was twelve, he was in several leagues, including a travel league bowling with kids well beyond his age. In fact, he was bowling with student-athletes from area high schools. He also played goalie in soccer, was a pitcher in Little League, and began boxing in the eighth grade. He never played football or threw the shot put.

When he was in the eighth grade, he came home with papers for high school football. He still wanted to continue to bowl, and was happy to find out that he could since football was a fall sport and bowling was a winter sport. He played football in the fall, bowled on the varsity team during the winter of his freshman year, and was in the weight room during the spring getting ready for football next season.

In his sophomore year, he again played football and was in the weight room the rest of the year (winter and spring seasons), getting ready for the next football season, which effectively replaced bowling. His junior year, he came home with papers for track and field: he wanted to throw the shot put, another new sport to replace the weight room. *Oh, good,* I thought. *He's in high school, and what better arena to learn and do new things?* Turns out he loved throwing the shot put and disk, and continued throughout his senior year throwing in both the winter and spring seasons. Football, bowling, track and field, and weight training represented his time in high school.

Each time he came home with papers for a different sport I would ask him the same question: "what does this entail?" Fortunately, I was somewhat familiar with each sport, so I didn't need him to explain the sport to me. His usual answer to my question was, "It's after school, Mom. Don't worry about it." And so I signed the papers.

After the first round of football freshman year, I knew that his assumption was not the case. It was never "just after school." We were thrown head-first into the wonderful world of high school sports. Suddenly we were dealing with coaches who were trying to do their jobs without the interference of parents; but I and other moms (some with previous high school sports experience) kept getting in the way. We wanted to know everything, just as we did with our sons' academic classes, just as we had prior to high school.

WHAT SPORT IS THIS?

If you are unfamiliar with the sport, make it a priority to learn, not only about the sport itself, but also the high school aspects of the sport. What time are games? Where are the games? Are games on weekends? When are practices? Are practices on weekends? And, most importantly, don't assume that there are no out-of-pocket expenses, just because it may be a public school.

Your knowledge will help keep your child safe and your stress levels down. Your understanding of the sport they want to play will also make conversations about practice and games more fun and interesting between you and your child. They'll feel as though you—the parent, the mom—are really interested, and you will discover that there's a new topic of interest that can be shared between the two of you. A big part of this new interest is understanding the level of commitment that's required.

COMMITMENT

Each of the different sports my son was involved in required a commitment from him, from me, and from his father.

> **Football**: Miles had to commit his summers to football. This meant that vacations were carefully planned so that he was back in time for football practice. This also altered his hopes of finding a part-time job. Finally, in September of his junior year, he found a job with a company that was willing to work around his academic and athletic schedules. He needed flexibility:

sometimes practice went overtime. Sometimes practices or games were rescheduled.

Bowling: Games and practices were right after school and he had to bring his own equipment with him to school. Try carrying three 16-pound bowling balls on the school bus! This meant that we had to drive him to and from school during bowling season.

Track and Field (shot put): Track meets were very long days. For winter track, they practiced many evenings. In the spring we sacrificed many weekends. One year, he planned a party with his friends, but due to a last-minute schedule change, the party he had been planning for several months had to be cancelled.

Weight Training: This was truly after school.

LESSONS YOUR CHILD CAN *LIVE* WITH

Lesson I — Be committed

Each sport requires a certain amount of time for practice and games. Make sure you understand how long this commitment is going to be for. Talk to your child. Can they handle this and schoolwork, along with other activities such as work, community service, and religious commitments?

This commitment is not just theirs: it is yours, too! Check your schedule.

Remind your student-athlete to commit to their health and nutritional needs as well.

"Each workout is like a brick in a building, and every time you go in there and do a half-ass workout, you're not laying a brick down. Somebody else is." Dorian Yates

Growing up as an athlete, I clearly understood the value of a committed team and of being committed to that team, as both an individual and as a teammate. Before the beginning of each season, Miles and I had the "commitment" talk. I would tell him that he needed to make the decision whether to stay on the team or not *before* the team was committed to him, at which point he had to see it through.

When your child comes home with paperwork seeking your approval for them to join a sport, don't just sign the paperwork: make sure that you understand the sport and the commitment that needs to be made to that sport. Don't ever assume that all sports require the same commitment! Some sports practice every day of the week; many teams practice on the weekends as well. Several fall sports start practice during the summer, leaving very little time for family vacations. Some winter sports practice during the winter break, and many spring sports practice during spring break. You should know this in advance so you don't plan a family vacation that conflicts with your child's commitments.

If your child is not invested in the sport, perhaps they should think twice about joining. Once your child has made the commitment, you too must be invested.

Many coaches hold at least one parent meeting at the beginning of the season. If you don't attend any other meeting, go to this one. Usually at this meeting the coach will hand out a copy of the schedule. If your son is like mine, the one the coach game him was *always* lost someplace in his backpack! At this meeting, the coach may also explain the expectations from both you and your child, along with what you can expect from him or her. If this information is not volunteered, you should raise the question.

What to do when you child wants to quit

If you allow your child to try different things (music lessons, several different sports, art lessons, etc.) as they grow up, you will easily know what they're good at ... and so will they!

It's always tough when your child comes home and says that they want to quit the team, drama club, marching band, or whatever it is that they're involved in. If you know that they're not talented in that discipline (be real, Mom: we know if our children can dance or not!), then the desire to quit is easier to accept.

But if you know they're talented in the area, you need to find out why they want to quit. Perhaps he's just tired of that activity. Maybe all her friends are joining the soccer team and she wants to do that too.

Regardless of the reason, make sure you talk to your child before you let them quit. It is important that they're making the decision because it is best for them. If you think they're quitting for the wrong reasons, try to point these out to them. Guide them through the pros and cons of quitting and starting something new.

Whenever my son wanted to try something new, we discussed the commitment and established a minimum period of time. When he was eight years old, he wanted to play the guitar. We didn't rush right out and buy him a guitar. We waited about three months to make sure this was what he really wanted to do. Knowing my son, if this was truly something he wanted to do, he would ask about it often.

And he did! For three months he constantly wanted to go to the music store and look at the guitars; he asked about lessons. When we felt he was ready, we found a very good local school and signed him up for six months of lessons. He understood from the beginning that he needed to make a six-month commitment. Why? Because we felt that was a reasonable amount of time for him to determine if he liked it or not. In the end, he took lessons for over two years. He discovered that he enjoyed music so much that he went on the play the trumpet, the alto and tenor saxophone, and now he raps and writes lyrics!

When he was in middle school, Miles played in the band for four years. Before the end of middle school, we reviewed what he was currently doing versus what he wanted to do in high school. Miles decided that he would put the instruments aside and do other things in high school. Thus prepared, when asked to continue playing the saxophone in the high school marching band, he was able to say no *before* making the commitment.

If you notice signs of diminished interest, such as not wanting to go to practice or a decrease in the level of enthusiasm, talk to your child and find out what is going on. Why the sudden lack of interest? There could be any number of reasons. If it's because they just don't like the coach, here is another life-lesson. We always want our children to be happy, but by the high school level they should understand that "disliking the coach" is not enough of a reason to quit, especially if they enjoy the sport or activity, or are talented in it.

Always review what is on your child's schedule. If the schedule is filled with extracurricular activities such as sports, work, community service, it is easy for them to become overwhelmed. Perhaps quitting some or all of the extracurricular activities is their way of getting things back under control.

Sit with your child and help them review their schedule. If it turns out that it is a team sport that they want to eliminate, my recommendation is to encourage them to finish out the season and honor their commitment to the coach and their teammates. However, if continuing with the sport will be detriment to them, set up a meeting to discuss their departure from the team with the coach. It's important that the coach understand why a player is leaving the team. It's important for us to teach our children how to depart with grace and respect.

Make sure they're quitting—not giving up!

Quitting versus giving up

If it's a choice between your child's physical or mental health, there is no choice. After playing football for three years, midway in his senior year, my son had to stop playing due to an injury involving his neck. This was not a choice. He had to stop playing, but he didn't quit the team or give up. He still went to practice and he went to all the remaining games of the season.

If your child is coming home distressed or depressed, here's another reason for you to step in and access the situation. Perhaps this particular sport is too demanding for your child and they're afraid to quit. In the end, *no* sport is worth our children's health.

However, if a physical or mental reason is not determined and your child still wants to quit, try to find out why (not always an easy task!). However, you should at least make sure that they quit a team or activity with respect. They should never just stop showing up. Closure is important. Remember that your child will still see the coach and teammates at school.

Student-athletes number one reason for quitting sports is because they're not having fun. Having fun is paramount in high school sports. Remember to always ask your child if they're having fun. You should be having fun, too!

THE ATHLETES' ATTITUDE

Short and sweet here, Mom: Know your child's personality and the changes in their attitude depending upon what they're doing and what is going on in their lives. This is the time in their lives when they learn what it means to have "grace" and to be "humble." Everyone loves the track star, but will *like* them if they present themselves as a nice person.

LESSONS YOUR CHILD *CAN LIVE* WITH

Lesson II — Respect others

It takes pride to respect others and it takes time to offer respect.

Being respectful is a sure way to say "thanks."

STATISTICS ABOUT HIGH SCHOOL SPORTS

The National Federation of State High School Associations is the national leadership organization for high school sports and fine arts activities. The primary task of the NFHS is to write the playing rules for high school sports.[1] The NFHS issued a press release on September 15, 2009, offering statistical information about school participation and student participation in high school sports.

NFHS Executive Director Robert F. Kanaby is quoted in the press release saying, "Given the state of the economy, this year's survey makes a great statement about the interest in high school sports in our nation's schools." Further he adds, "The record participation levels for boys and girls reflect the fact that participation in high school sports is of great value to our nation's young people. Also, the survey's results support the NFHS 2008—2011 Strategic Plan, in which the organization vowed to provide stronger leadership for high school athletics and fine arts activities."[2]

Participation in high school sports is at a record high despite reduced funding in high schools across the country. The number of athletes has steadily increased over the past 20

---

[1] *"High School Sports Participation Increases for 20th Consecutive Year"* Press Release issued September 15, 2009. Found at nfhs.org/content.aspx?id=3505

[2] *"High School Sports Participation Increases for 20th Consecutive Year"* Press Release issued September 15, 2009. nfhs.org/content.aspx?id=3505

years. In the 2008-09 school year, 7,536,753 high school students participated in sports. Boys reached a high of 4,422,662 and girls increased by 56,825. In fact, girls went from 294,015 participating in 1971-72, to 3,114,091 in 2008-09. Based upon the survey, 55.2 percent of the students enrolled in high school participate in athletics, a slight increase from the previous year of 54.8 percent.[3]

---

[3] *"High School Sports Participation Increases for 20th Consecutive Year"* Press Release issued September 15, 2009. nfhs.org/content.aspx?id=3505

The following chart list the top ten sports played in high school during the 2008-09 school year for both boys and girls. It also includes the number of athletes that participated in each sport.

NATIONAL FEDERATION OF STATE HIGH SCHOOL ASSOCIATIONS[4]
2008-09 ATHLETICS PARTICIPATION SUMMARY

TEN MOST POPULAR BOYS PROGRAMS

	Schools			Participants	
1	Basketball	17,869	1	Football - 11 player	1,112,303
2	Track and Field - Outdoor	15,936	2	Track and Field - Outdoor	558,007
3	Baseball	15,699	3	Basketball	545,145
4	Football - 11 player	14,105	4	Baseball	473,184
5	Cross Country	13,647	5	Soccer	383,824
6	Golf	13,543	6	Wrestling	267,378
7	Soccer	11,139	7	Cross Country	231,452
8	Wrestling	10,254	8	Tennis	157,165
9	Tennis	9,499	9	Golf	157,062
10	Swimming and Diving	6,556	10	Swimming and Diving	130,182

TEN MOST POPULAR GIRLS PROGRAMS

	Schools			Participants	
1	Basketball	17,582	1	Track and Field - Outdoor	457,732
2	Track and Field - October	15,864	2	Basketball	444,809
3	Softball - Fast Pitch	15,172	3	Volleyball	404,243
4	Volleyball	15,069	4	Softball - Fast Pitch	368,921
5	Cross Country	13,457	5	Soccer	344,534
6	Soccer	10,548	6	Cross Country	198,199
7	Tennis	9,693	7	Tennis	177,593
8	Golf	9,344	8	Swimming and Diving	158,878
9	Swimming and Diving	6,902	9	Competitive Spirit Squads	117,793
10	Competitive Spirit Squads	4,748	10	Golf	69,223

The complete survey is available on the NFHS website at nhfs.com.

---

[4] *"High School Sports Participation Increases for 20th Consecutive Year"* Press Release issued September 15, 2009. nfhs.org/content.aspx?id=3505

So, Your Child Wants to Play High School Sports!

The next chart, lead by Texas, shows the rank by state of the number of athletes that played high school sports during the 2008-09 school year.

2008-09 SUMMARY OF ATHLETICS PARTICIPATION TOTALS BY STATE

Rank	State	Boys	Girls	Total[5]
1	Texas	475,770	305,230	781,000
2	California	443,154	328,311	771,465
3	New York	217,566	163,304	380,870
4	Illinois	205,396	136,367	341,763
5	Ohio	203,631	126,425	330,056
6	Pennsylvania	173,059	148,265	321,324
7	Michigan	181,642	129,635	311,277
8	New Jersey	150,283	107,515	257,798
9	Florida	141,031	101,325	242,356
10	Minnesota	120,689	103,531	224,220
11	Massachusetts	120,341	92,433	212,774
12	Wisconsin	118,741	79,710	198,451
13	Missouri	107,707	76,211	183,918
14	North Carolina	103,820	78,384	182,204
15	Virginia	100,206	71,549	171,755
16	Georgia	107,390	63,192	170,582
17	Indiana	93,557	63,417	156,974
18	Iowa	85,681	64,537	150,218
19	Washington	82,882	58,604	141,486
20	Colorado	70,825	55,536	126,361
21	Maryland	64,704	46,398	111,102
22	Connecticut	61,652	48,299	109,951
23	Tennessee	69,067	37,728	106,795
24	Arizona	65,763	40,146	105,909
25	Kansas	62,488	39,889	102,377
26	Mississippi	64,832	36,656	101,488
27	Kentucky	54,667	43,803	98,470
28	Oregon	57,963	39,193	97,156
29	South Carolina	56,419	33,532	89,951
30	Alabama	59,398	28,410	87,808
31	Louisiana	46,721	34,392	81,113

[5] Reflects participation rate, i.e., individual who participated in two sports is counted twice, three sports – three times, etc. *"High School Sports Participation Increases for 20th Consecutive Year"* Press Release issued September 15, 2009. nfhs.org/content.aspx?id=3505 – link within the press release

32	Nebraska	47,046	31,911	78,957
33	Oklahoma	43,068	32,356	75,424
34	Arkansas	38,173	24,790	62,963
35	Maine	30,683	26,558	57,241
36	Utah	31,446	19,926	51,372
37	New Mexico	28,192	20,312	48,504
38	Idaho	27,327	19,736	47,063
39	New Hampshire	24,451	21,980	46,431
40	Nevada	25,563	15,847	41,410
41	Hawaii	21,795	15,770	37,565
42	West Virginia	21,991	15,338	37,329
43	Montana	18,700	14,256	32,956
44	South Dakota	17,218	11,987	29,205
45	Rhode Island	16,621	12,205	28,826
46	Delaware	14,732	11,114	25,846
47	North Dakota	14,899	10,669	25,568
48	Alaska	11,367	9,742	21,109
49	Vermont	10,113	8,482	18,595
50	Wyoming	10,104	7,923	18,027
51	District of Columbia	2,178	1,262	3,440

WHAT YOU SHOULD KNOW ABOUT HIGH SCHOOL ATHLETICS

High school sports are played in three seasons:

- fall
- winter
- spring

Following is a list of sports and when they may be offered. Depending upon the size of the school and school district, what is offered for *your* child may be different. However, the seasons are usually consistent since schools in different districts play against each other.

Fall	Winter	Spring
Football	Basketball	Baseball
Tennis	Swimming	Softball
Cross-country	Wrestling	Track & field
Soccer	Track & field	Golf
Field hockey	Bowling	Tennis
Gymnastics	Cheerleading	Lacrosse
Cheerleading	Ice Hockey	Weightlifting
Volleyball	Skiing	

Aside from these, there may also be a dance team, step team, and color guard (which perform with the marching band). Knowing what is offered and when it is offered can help you help your child plan. In some cases a choice will need to be made.

Playing several sports is not for all children and their families. It's very easy to get sports burnout. I have a friend who gets sports burnout every year. By the middle of October, she is ready to throw in the towel. "It's too much!" she laments. Between the practices, games, additional laundry, extra food, and increased spending, she is happy that her son only plays soccer.

To help me plan better (an important survival skill!), I use highschoolsports.net. This website not only shows the scheduled times for games and practices, it also lists the team they're playing, where they're playing, and provides directions. Make sure you keep this website handy, just in case your child forgets to tell you they've a game or where the game is!

OTHER PARENTS

Sometimes other parents can be the biggest problem you encounter. It will not take long for you to figure out which parents should be avoided! Sitting on the other side of the bleachers can help you to enjoy the game. We've all heard the expression "soccer mom." Well, the soccer mom goes to football and baseball games too! There is a good chance that you are a soccer mom and don't realize it.

What is a Soccer Mom?

It was in 1990 that the phrase "soccer mom" became popular. "Soccer mom" refers to a woman (a mom) who spends a great deal of her time being involved with her children's sports activities. She makes it clear that her family and children come first.

Her activities may include transporting her children and yours from one sporting event to the next, calling other moms to reschedule meetings, attending booster club meeting or arranging which moms will work the stand at half-time. At the game she is totally absorbed by the magnificent feats her child can perform and is known to be quite vocal at times during the games. You know who she is! Remember the last game when you could not resist looking over your shoulder to see who was screaming so loudly?

WHAT TO DO WHEN YOUR CHILD DOESN'T WANT TO PLAY HIGH SCHOOL SPORTS

Don't force your child to play a sport in high school. There are a great number of other opportunities available for your child to get involved in. We all have our dreams for our children, but whether or not they play high school sports needs to be *their* dream—not our dream for them.

If you have two children in high school, and one doesn't want to play sports, don't draw comparisons between the two siblings. Refrain from saying things like, "why don't you want to play basketball like your sister?" For the one that wants to play, that's great. You should encourage them and be there for them.

For the one that *doesn't* want to play sports, first ask them why they don't want to play sports, especially if they've participated in sports prior to high school. Maybe the high school level is too competitive for them; perhaps they've lost interest in sports; or perhaps they're really just undecided. In this situation, you should sit with them and review all the athletic and other activities that they can be involved in. Point out to them that participating in extracurricular activities in high school helps to make the high school experience that much more rewarding. Don't give up, but don't push too hard. Let the child make the decision.

Don't try to push your children into playing high sports because they can get a scholarship to college. With over seven million children playing high school sports, only about 1.2 percent will receive an athletic scholarship for college; and for many, the scholarship rarely covers 100 percent of the cost of college. In Chapter 16, *Playing at the Next Level*, we talk about this subject in greater detail.

2 - WHO IS REALLY IN CHARGE?

*The coach may be responsible for your
son during practice and games.
The athletic trainer may care for your daughter's
ankle by wrapping it before the game.
But ultimately you, Mom, are in charge 24/7!*

There are a lot of different terms to describe the sports parent, but for me "Mom" says it all.

WHO IS MOM?

Females outnumber males in the United States by over six million (roughly six percent) and a significant percent have at least one child. There are 141,606,000 women with children in the United States.[6] This means that at some point, a majority of these children will be in high school, and roughly 55 percent or 77,883,000 will enjoy high school sports.

The Mom's Day

Maria T. Bailey, author of *Moms 3.0,* points out that "moms are doing more than spending money. We are engaged in everything from washing clothes to budgeting business plans. We are online, offline and off-road. Moms are chatting, tweeting and blogging with friends, family and strangers. One thing we all have in common is that we are time-starved."

How on earth can we fit high school sports into our already busy schedules? According to BSM Media research, 64 percent of moms say they've given up sleep in order to get work/chores done so that they could spend time with their children.[7] I'm guilty of this! I'll do laundry in the middle of the night so that I can go to the game the next day. Our scheduling dilemma is not an excuse for us to put the coach in charge of our children. Don't send your child to baseball practice and ask that their little brother also go. Baseball practice is not a

---

[6] Bureau of the Census, Population of the United States by Age, Sex, Race and Hispanic Origin: 1993 to 2050, Washington D.C.: GPO, 1996 Business Research, Women-Owned Business in the United States, 2002: A Fact Sheet. (Found in *Mom 3.0* by Maria T. Bailey, page 38. Mom 3.0 is Published by Wyatt-MacKenzie Publishing, Inc.)
[7] *Mom 3.0* by Maria Bailey, page 39. Published by Wyatt-MacKenzie Publishing, Inc.

babysitter. It is also not fair to the child who's playing the sport and can be a distraction to the rest of the team.

We are also very good with a camera. We record everything. And we have opinions. If we like the coach, all our friends will know. If we don't like the coach, everybody will know. With everything that we do, our children should still be our primary focus. This priority doesn't change just because they play high school sports.

Bailey further states that 40percent of today's moms chat and socialize with other moms online. While online, we are sharing information with others—and empowering ourselves to do more—with less time. About 30 percent of us have blogged and 66 percent have posted a message on a board or chatted online. With all of this going on, if Mom is pleased or displeased with her child's high school sports activities, she's talking about it.

Eighty percent of all checks written in the United States are signed by women.[8] This leads us to assume that majority of the papers filled out for high school sports will be filled out by the moms, including the numerous order forms for team apparel. This means that Mom has to be comfortable with the sport(s) their children want to play.

---

[8] Faith Popcorn, EVEolution: Under Women: Eight Essential Truths That Work in Your Business and Life, (Dimensions, 2001). (Found in *Mom 3.0* by Maria T. Bailey, page 39. Published by Wyatt-MacKenzie Publishing, Inc)

We share ... a *lot*. Sixty-four percent of us ask other moms for advice before making a purchase. We are efficient and usually plan ahead. In fact, fifty percent of us have Halloween planned prior to Labor Day, and sixty-five percent have thought about our fall calendar by the first day of school.[9] Not surprisingly, this means that we are also planning our schedules for fall sports by midsummer. As we draw closer to September, I find myself, along with the other football moms, talking and getting ready for the season.

Moms share everything from complaining about the cost of the varsity jacket to their children's injuries to how they feel about the coach. If you are a freshman mom, befriend an upperclassman's mom, and see how fast you are no longer feeling new.

Moms' Core Values[10]

According to Marie T. Bailey, there are five core values that all moms share, regardless of age, race, ethnicity, family size, or geographical location. We (moms) use these values to ensure our children grow up safe and healthy, with the hope of having "more"—whether it's food or education, in the most

---

[9] *Mom 3.0* by Maria T. Bailey, page 40. Published by Wyatt-MacKenzie Publishing, Inc.
[10] *Mom 3.0*, by Maria T. Bailey, page 22. Published by Wyatt-MacKenzie Publishing, Inc.

value-minded simplistic way possible within our limited
amount of time.

- Health and safety
- Family enrichment
- Value
- Simplification
- Time management

LESSONS YOUR CHILD CAN *LIVE* WITH

Lesson III — Who is Mom and Who is the Coach?

Make sure your child understands who is who, and the differences. You, Mom, are always in charge, and should not be kept in the dark as it pertains to your child's wellbeing.

The high school coach is responsible for them as it pertains to a particular sport. The coach can—and *should*—be a positive role model for our children. A good coach helps to instill discipline and self-worth in the players on their team, but they're not there to mother them.

A great coach can be a lifetime friend.

It's important that our children understand the difference between mothering and coaching:

Mothering

The nurturing and raising of a child or children by a mother.[11]

Life-lasting relationships are developed between coaches and athletes. For example, I remained in contact with my high school dance coach for over 20 years! She didn't replace my mother, but she was another positive female role model in my life. This is important to understand. It's your responsibility to learn who the coach is. This person will have an effect on your child's life. What you want is for this to be a *positive* effect!

Helicopter Mom

I loved being a "helicopter mom!" It was fun, it was exciting, and it kept me busy. Of course now that my son is eighteen years old, I have changed seats with him and now he's the pilot!

So what exactly is a helicopter parent? The term is used to describe a parent that pays extremely close attention to their child's experiences and problems, particularly at

---

[11] thefreedictionary.com/mothering

educational institutions. The term was originated by Foster W. Cline, M.D., and Jim Fay in their 1990 book *Parenting with Love and Logic: Teaching Children Responsibility*. Helicopter parents are so named because, like helicopters, we hover closely overhead, rarely out of reach, whether our children need us or not.[12]

Yes, that was me. Is it you? Now think of a coach having one, two, or even 10 helicopter moms to deal with. I think it was football that forced me to begin to let go, that and the fact that my son would be leaving for college in less than one year. Although I still hover, I am across the river looking through binoculars.

Funny, I think I see more.

Remember: Just because our children are seventeen or eighteen years of age, because they're driving and have part-time jobs, doesn't mean that we are no longer a part of their lives. They're still our children in high school. It is your job as the "mom" to make sure the coach knows that *you* are in still in charge, and involved, and willing to support him and the team.

---

[12] http://en.wikipedia.org/wiki/Helicopter_mom / Cline, Foster W.; Fay, Jim (1990), "*Parenting with Love and Logic: Teaching Children Responsibility*," Pinon Press, pp. 23–25, ISBN 0-89109-311-7, loveandlogic.com

WORLD'S TOUGHEST JOB[13]

If they wrote a help-wanted ad for the job of parenting, who would have the guts to apply?

JOB DESCRIPTION OF A PARENT

POSITION: Mom, Mommy, Mama, Ma

Dad, Daddy, Dada, Pa, Pop

JOB DESCRIPTION: Long-term team players needed for challenging permanent work in an often chaotic environment. Candidates must possess excellent communication and organizational skills and be willing to work variable hours, which will include evenings and weekends and frequent 24-hour shifts on call.

Some overnight travel required, including trips to primitive camping sites on rainy weekends and endless sports tournaments in far-away cities. Travel expenses not reimbursed. Extensive courier duties also required.

---

[13] *"Job Description for Parents,"* by Annette Clifford, was originally published in Florida Today in Melbourne, Florida.
"World's Toughest Job" by Annette Clifford available at worldstoughtstjob.com.

RESPONSIBILITIES: Must provide on-the-site training in basic life skills such as nose-blowing. Must be willing to be hated, at least temporarily, until someone needs five dollars. Must be willing to bite tongue repeatedly. Must possess the physical stamina of a pack mule and be able to go from zero to 60 mph in three seconds flat (in case, this time, the screams from the backyard are not someone just crying wolf).

Must be willing to face stimulating technical challenges, such as small-gadget repair, mysteriously sluggish toilets, and stuck zippers. Must screen phone calls, maintain calendars, and coordinate production of multiple homework projects. Must have ability to plan and organize social gatherings for clients of all ages and mental outlooks. Must be willing to be indispensable one minute, an embarrassment the next.

Must handle assembly and product safety testing of a half million cheap plastic toys and battery-operated devices. Must always hope for the best but be prepared for the worst. Must assume final, complete accountability for the quality of the end product.

Responsibilities also include floor maintenance and janitorial work throughout the facility.

POSSIBILITY FOR ADVANCEMENT/PROMOTION: None. Your job is to remain in the same position for years, without complaining, constantly retraining and updating your skills, so that those in your charge can ultimately surpass you.

PREVIOUS EXPERIENCE: None required, unfortunately. On-the-job training offered on a continual, exhausting basis.

WAGES AND COMPENSATION: Get this! *You* pay *them*! Must offer frequent raises and bonuses.

A balloon payment is due when they turn 18 because of the assumption that college will help them become financially independent. When you die, you give them whatever is left. The oddest thing about this reverse-salary scheme is that you actually enjoy it and only wish you could do more.

BENEFITS: While no health or dental insurance, no pension, no tuition reimbursement, no paid holidays and no stock options are offered, this job supplies limitless opportunities for personal growth and free hugs and kisses for life if you play your cards right.

SURVIVAL KIT

Your survival kit is in the trunk of your car. I clean out my trunk every June and refill it in September, just before the start of the football season. I recommend you pack it all at once, because a cold evening at a football game can sneak up on you. When I cleaned it out in June, I would put everything in a bin; that way I knew where everything was. Here is a list of some of the items you may want to consider keeping in your survival kit:

- seat cushions: every high school stadium is different, but they all have one thing in common: the bleachers are hard!
- blankets: I use them mostly to wrap my legs and ankles. The wind always manages to whip around me in the bleachers, especially since I like to sit high up.
- sweatshirt, jacket or sweater: school colors, of course!
- hat, scarf, and gloves.
- umbrella and/or rain gear.
- boots: you may have to walk through mud or dirt to get to the bleachers.
- folding chair: quite frequently, the bleachers

for visitors are half the size of the home
bleachers. Just so you don't have to stand
the entire game, have your own chair.

- book and/or magazine: sometimes you will
  find that you are sitting around waiting.
- towel: great just in case it rains and you or the
  bleachers get wet.
- a tool kit: you never know!
- first-aid kit: although the team has a first aid
  kit, it never hurts to be prepared for when your child
  gets in the car.
- snacks: just something to hold you over. I
  usually carried pretzels or trail mix.

THE HANK GATHERS STORY

Eric "Hank" Gathers was a college basketball player at
Loyola Marymount University who collapsed and died during
a game in 1990. In 1992, his story was made into the move
Final Shot: The Hank Gathers Story.

On December 9, 1989, Gathers collapsed at the free-
throw line during a Loyola Marymount University home game
against University of California, Santa Barbara. He was
diagnosed with an abnormal heartbeat (exercise-induced

ventricular tachycardia), and was given a beta blocker. The purpose of the beta blocker was to inhibit the effects of adrenaline and smooth the heart's rhythms.

On March 4, 1990, he collapsed again and died at the young age of 23. An autopsy found that he suffered from a heart-muscle disorder called hypertrophic cardiomyopathy.[14]

This is a tragic and unfortunate incident. We have heard of other unfortunate stores such this one. Who is to say what can and cannot be prevented when our children go away to college? Once they're at college, we no longer have control over what they do—we aren't there to verify that medications are being taken, or that they're correctly following doctor's orders. We don't know if they've informed the athletic trainer or team doctor of all injuries, ailments, or conditions, not to mention medications they take, including cold medicines and other over-the-counter drugs.

But we do have control at the high school level.

---

[14] Hypertrophic cardiomyopathy: A genetic disorder of the heart characterized by increased thickness (hypertrophy) of the wall of the left ventricle, the largest of the four chambers of the heart. The disease can present at any time in life. It is the leading cause of sudden death in athletes and young people. Abbreviated HCM. It is inherited in an autosomal dominant manner. Men and women with HCM stand a 50-50 chance of transmitting the HCM gene to each of their children. MedicineNet.com.
medterms.com/script/main/art.asp?articlekey=7845

As an athlete myself, I understand playing through pain. As a dancer I have performed with pulled muscles, knee injuries, shin splints, and a bruised pelvis from a fall. Why? Because if I didn't perform, someone else was always waiting in the wings to take my spot! Not an excuse, just reality. Someone taking "your spot" is one of an athlete's biggest fears.

Case in point

In 2001, inexperienced Tom Brady replaced New England Patriots quarterback Drew Bledsoe after he suffered a devastating hit from New York Jets linebacker Mo Lewis. Although Bledsoe recovered, Head Coach Bill Belichick allowed Brady to keep the starting position because he'd played so well. The Patriots finished the season with an 11 to five record and went on to defeat the St. Louis Rams 20-17 in Super Bowl XXXVI. Brady was named Super Bowl MVP and Bledsoe was traded to the Buffalo Bills during the following off-season.

3 – I'LL BE THERE!

Second-hand news is old news!

In today's world of electronics it is a magic trick to not be there, to not be involved. You don't always need to be there in the flesh, but you should make sure your son or daughter knows that you are with them.

I travel as a part of my career, but whenever possible I am at the game. However, there are times when business calls and I am out of town. When this happens, I text my son a short note, "Good luck," and I call him later that evening after the game to hear how he and his team fared. I am there, and he knows it. I have also befriended several other moms who keep watch for me. One of my closest friends, Sandy, whose son played football with mine would Facebook® me and tell me how my son did … and her son, too!

When I was growing up, my parents were always there for me. For the good—*and* the not-so-good performances. One theatre performance, I sang an entire song in the wrong key. Embarrassing? You bet! Afterward, my mother told me that I sang beautifully in the key of my choice.

As an athlete growing up, I can tell you first-hand that one of the best feelings in the world is to look out into the stands and see your parents there. Many children won't complain about their parents not being there to their friends or parents; however, I have heard many make excuses for their parents' absence. They say things like, "my mom was busy." My question is, "busy doing what?" If you are getting your nails done, change the appointment. If you are home cooking dinner, eat a little later. Your presence at the games cannot be replaced. Even thought I stay in touch when I travel, I still feel as though I missed out.

At the end of a football game or track meet, my son is hungry first, tired second, and grumpy third (probably because of the first two); but he always says thanks to me for being there to take him home. The summer months were difficult for football practice. I could get him there, but I could not pick him up afterward because I was at work almost an hour away.

"Anthony's mom will bring you home," I would tell him.

"I know, but it's not the same" he would reply.

How long will this last? I would wonder. If I could just make it through high school with him still wanting to spend time with me and wanting me there, I'll survive college. Now as I write this, my son has less than six months before he is off to college, and I know that because of the relationship I have had with him, because of all the great experiences we have shared and the number of games I have watched him play, I'll survive his absence while he is away at college. I also know that he values his health beyond any sport and will not put himself at risk.

GET INVOLVED

Since you are there, you may as well get involved. If you are involved with your child's studies, why aren't you involved with their sports activities in high school? If you know their teachers by sight and by name, why don't you know the coach by sight or by name? Statistics say that children of parents who are actively involved with their studies do better in the classroom.

If you are involved with your child's sports, he or she will also have greater success. By success I don't mean they'll be the number-one star player on the team, or win every game they play, but rather that they will strive to be the best they can be at that particular sport ... because you will love them and be proud of them no matter what; and they will applaud their own efforts.

Let's define "involved." Being at the game is not being involved. Helping the team is being involved. Every sports program needs help and money. There is no such thing as "they have enough." New updated equipment is needed; uniforms wear out and need be fixed or replaced.

A volunteer is worth twenty pressed men![15]
Proverb

Being involved is also a great way for you to get to know other parents, especially if you work. Having made a few friends made my life easier.

---

[15] Proverb: "*A volunteer is worth twenty pressed men.*" Someone who volunteers for military duty would perform twenty better than someone who was drafted or "pressed" into service. Found at phrases.org.uk/bulletin_board/9/messages/418.html

"LESSONS YOUR CHILD CAN *LIVE* WITH"

Lesson IV — Be involved

We raise our children in hopes that they will one day become parents and have a better life than we gave them. That they will be good parents and hopefully involved in their children's lives.

If we are not involved in their lives, how can we expect that they'll be any different?

The German proverb "Der Apfel fällt nicht weit vom Stamm" (the apple doesn't fall far from the tree) stands true for all cultures. In so many ways, our children become who we are. We start out by saying, "I'll never be like my mother," and then one day wake up and say "I'm so like my mother!"

This carries over into how involved we are in our children's lives, and includes sports. If you want your child to grow up to be an involved parent, you need to be an involved parent.

Fundraising

In most schools, fundraising is necessary for athletic programs to survive. The schools only have a certain amount of money allocated for each sport. Booster clubs and parents' associations have been developed to help fill the financial gap needed to help defray out-of-pocket expenses. The more parents get involved, the less work each will need to do. Sometimes, it is as simple as selling raffle tickets or working the stand at half time.

Certain sports such as cheerleading not only cheer at football and basketball games, but frequently participate in competitions; and many go to cheer camp as a group during the summer months. Often these competitions are in another state and new uniforms are ordered. This is where getting involved helps. If there is an active parent group or booster club that can raise money, some of these additional costs can be covered. If not, most likely you will have to pay for all additional activities out of your pocket.

More often than not, it is less than five percent of all the parents that get involved; but a far greater percentage than that complain about how things are being done. I have experienced this first-hand. For over two years I worked as the vice president of the parents' association for my son's football team, and during that time, approximately six of us did the majority of the work. Note there were over 80 boys involved with the football program!

4 – A MOM'S SURVEY

A rewarding experience for our children!
A rewarding experience for us and our families!
We are and will always be our children's
biggest cheerleaders!

A MOM'S SURVEY

I gave several moms who have children playing high school sports—or have children who played high school sports in the past—a survey. I would like to share some of the results with you. I also took the survey and my responses are marked MW.

Q.   *As a parent of a high school athlete, what one or two things did you learn about high school athletics while your child participated?*

A1.   Parents are sometimes more competitive than their children and some children react to losing a game better than their parents.

A2.   Too intense and too demanding.

A3.   It is a lot of time the kids must give up and sometimes they get nothing in return.

A4.   Politics.

MW.   It took more of my time than I realized it would.

Q.   *What preconceived ideas did you have that were proven incorrect?*

A.   That everyone gets a chance to play.

MW.   That practice would end in time for my son to get the late bus home. In the early years, before he and his friends started driving, many days I had to rush from work, or try to find someone to bring him home or back to school in time for the bus.

Q.   *What did you dislike about high school athletics?*

A1.   The politics.

A2.   The amount of time it takes.

A3.   Too intense and too demanding.

A4.   The win at all cost attitude.

A5.   Even if the student never missed a practice they were not given the opportunity to play.

A6.   The lack of parental involvement.

MW.   Sometimes the away games were a bit far.

Q.   *What did you like about high school athletics?*

A.   The bonding. My daughter made lots of new friends.

MW.   Not only did my son get to meet and interact with kids he may never have the chance to, but I too got to make a few very good friends.

Q.   *What changes or improvements would you recommend to your son or daughter's high school?*

A1.   More focused on fun.

A2.   Allow all players a chance to play.

A3.   Explain the timeline in advance. It was difficult to plan vacations.

MW.   Offer a meeting at the beginning of each season to talk with parents about the expectations of high school sports.

Q.   *As a parent of a high school athlete what was your greatest fear?*

A.   That my son would get injured beyond repair.

MW. Aside from injury, I didn't want my son to let his personality get too caught up in sports.

Q.   *Approximately how much money did you spend on uniforms, travel, shoes, etc. for each sport?*

A.   Answers ranged from $100 to $500 per sport.

MW. I spent on the average $350 to $500 per sport.

Q.   *Did your son or daughter's grades change when they were playing sports?*

A.   Most said no. Those who said yes indicated that the grades changed for the worst.

MW. As a freshman, my son was too tired to do his homework and his grades suffered. By the time he was a junior, he had developed a system that worked well for him.

Q.   *What percentage of home games did you attend?*

A.   The answers ranged from 20 percent to 90 percent for both home and away games.

MW.   Unless I was traveling for work I attended home games, and majority of the away games.

Q.   *What advice would you give to the parent of a high school freshman?*

A1.   Support your child.

A2.   Remember that it is your child's efforts and love for the sport.

A3.   Let your child choose what they want to play.

A4.   Don't try to relieve any unfulfilled myths of your own through your child.

A5.   Make sure your child is having fun.

A6.   Don't force your child to play sports.

MW.   Get involved!

Q.   *Can you share a positive story?*

A1.   When my son comes off the field and shares with me that everyone was treated equal at practice today and he gives me a big smile.

A2.   When my daughter played her last game in high school I cried because I knew it was my last game too. Now my grandchildren will some day carry on the tradition.

MW   I really enjoy the game when I can see that the players who may not be the best get a chance to play.

Our children have a life after high school. If you treat them, or allow them to behave, like high school is the end of their life, it will be difficult for them when high school is over.

5 – FINANCIAL RESPONSIBILITY
It's worth every penny!

There is always a cost. If your child is in a public school, you probably don't pay for your child to participate. In many sports—such as football, baseball, and basketball—the uniforms are provided by the school; but there are many sports where you need to help subsidize the cost of the uniform.

And don't forget practice clothes for all sports!

My son played three sports in high school that required out-of-pocket expenses: football, bowling and track and field. On the average, we spent $1100 to $1500 per school year, or $4400 to $6000 over four years. Sound like a lot? It really isn't, once you break down all the cost involved. Several of the costs are small, but frequent, such as the cup of hot chocolate my husband and I purchased at football games.

Become budget-savvy for high school sports!

If you understand the cost, you can manage the cost. Just as you manage the expenses for your household, you need to mange the expenses for high school sports. By developing a budget, you'll know what you will need and when you need it. Some sports, like cheerleading and track and field, are enjoyed during more than one season. This can help cut down on the yearly expenses.

Before you sign on the dotted line and allow your child to participate in a sport, make sure you understand the cost involved!

I remember attending my son's first varsity football game. I got to the gate and needed to purchase a ticket. No one told me that there was a charge to see my son play football. It was only four dollars, but that adds up: over eight to ten games during the season, I ended up spending between thirty-two and forty dollars.

"LESSONS YOUR CHILD *CAN LIVE* WITH"

Lesson V — It takes money

Let your children know that their participation in sports has a financial value. Don't make them feel guilty about this value. In fact, make sure to tell them that you love that they're playing sports and don't mind the financial commitment.

As long as they, too, stay committed.

BUDGETING FOR HIGH SCHOOL SPORTS

Here is a list of items you may want to plan for. Depending upon the sport, some items may or may not pertain to your child; and some are given to your child by the team. As you will see from this list, reaching the $1,100 mark annually is not that hard if your child participates in three sports per school year.

I remember my first spring track meet. It was all day on a very hot day. I spent $20.00 on food and water!

<u>Here is a list of expenses you may need to budget for:</u>
- personal sports equipment
- shoes and socks
- varsity jacket
- team bag
- team jacket
- team pictures
- team items sold by the booster club: sweatshirts, hats, blankets, etc.
- raffle tickets and 50/50s
- transportation for you and your family to attend the games
- food and beverages that you purchase during the game for you and your family
- food and beverages that your athlete purchases before or during the game
- admission to varsity games
- game programs
- medical expenses if your child needs to go to the doctor due to an injury from playing
- annual sports physical. (many school districts offer this for free as an option)
- camps

- volunteering expenses, such as cooking for the team
- school fee to play. Due to budget cuts and restrictions, many school required that parents pay a fee for their children to play high school sports

Vacation Planning

It becomes quite costly if you have to cancel a vacation in order for your child to attend a sporting event. A friend of mine has a daughter whose team was traveling to another state for a competition. This cost the family an additional $1000 in travel, hotel and food for the mother and daughter to attend, along with the cost of having to cancel the planned vacation for the mother and daughter.

So plan ahead! Learn not only the school schedule, but the schedule for the competitions if your child's team should advance to the next level. You want to be there! But it will take money, so start planning now.

6 – THE HIGH SCHOOL PRINCIPAL AND THE ATHLETIC DIRECTOR
Communication is key!

THE PRINCIPAL

The principal is a professional educator who has the responsibility for the day-to-day operation, supervision of all school activities involving students, teachers, and other school personnel, and management and control of a particular school. The guidelines for the principal and his or her school are established by the school board (also known as the board of education).

The principal is usually not a coach, athletic trainer, or the athletic director, although many have coached high school sports in the past. In a very small school district, you may find that the principal is in fact a coach and assumes many of the duties of the athletic director.

THE ATHLETIC DIRECTOR

The athletic director is not the principal or the athletic trainer. In some smaller school districts, that person may also be a coach. Like the principal, the athletic director is a professional educator whose areas of responsibility pertain directly to the athletic programs and activities of the school(s) they're assigned. This responsibility is assumed for all sports, including varsity and intramural, along with the entire physical education program.

You may see them at various athletic events, and they appear to have nothing to do but stand around and watch. This is far from the truth! They're there to help ensure that everything runs smoothly. Some athletic directors are also responsible for athletic equipment, the coordination of transportation to and from games, and the officials for the games. Depending on the school district, they're also responsible for handling this for more than one high school. At one point in time the athletic director was a teacher, guidance counselor, coach, or all three.

An effective athletic director will provide leadership to the coaches and physical education teachers. They offer guidance to ensure that all athletic programs are run according to regulations, both state and local.

If you have a problem with the coach and cannot resolve it with him or her, speak with the athletic director before you go to the principal about the issue. In most cases the situation can be resolved at that level.

For the most part, it is a thankless job done by a group of people who love high school sports.

Lastly, it is not the responsibility of the athletic director to help your child get a college scholarship. If funding permits, they may offer a night of college recruiting. In any case, they're a great source of information, so don't be afraid to ask their advice!

AN ATHLETIC DIRECTOR'S PERSPECTIVE

What is on the mind of an athletic director? I wanted to know, so I asked.

Athletic Director Profile:

- Currently athletic director for two high schools
- Former coach
- Parent of student-athletes

• Former high school student-athlete

• Former college lacrosse player

• Former professional lacrosse player

Q.   *If you were speaking to a group of parents about what to look forward to in high school sports, what would you tell them? This can include whatever you think is important and what you think will help make your job as the athletic director easier, and their experience a positive one.*

A.   Be supportive of their son or daughter and be supportive of the coach and their program. Often parents will "Monday-morning quarterback," a head coach's philosophy, practice schedule, or game strategy. When this is done, it sends a confusing message to the student-athlete and can create issues within a program.

Have fun! At the high school level it seems as if we replace the word "fun" with "win." This should not be the case.

Be realistic! One of the hardest issues to tackle is helping a student-athlete recognize their potential and keep that potential in prospective. Not all students are going pro or getting a division-one scholarship. They are, however, going to college for an education, let's not lose site of that goal.

Communicate with the your child's coach and follow the chain of communication when an issue arises. Be open and honest.

Q. *What do you enjoy most about being a high school athletic director?*

A. Watching the progression in a young person as they mature from grade nine through twelve.

Q. *Which aspects of your job take the most time?*

A. 1. Day-to-day operations, scheduling buses and officials.
    2. Budgeting and inventory.
    3. Observation and evaluation.

Q. *What is the most rewarding aspect of being a high school athletic director?*

A. Again, student achievement.

Q. *How does being a high school athletic director affect your family?*

A. Positive involvement with my family. My son's came with me to the games.
    Negative: I am working six days a week when in season, which affects vacations.

Q. *What is the hardest aspect of being a high school athletic director?*

A. Letting a coach go due to lack of productivity, and dealing with student-athletes and their parents after tryouts and cuts.

Q.   *What would you change?*

A.   Communication between all parties involved in high school athletics.

7 – THE COACH

Not the parent, athletic director,
athletic trainer, or doctor

Coaching

The ability to support, teach and assist.

Many times the coach is also a teacher who has all his or her teaching responsibilities on top of any coaching responsibilities.

Before the first practice, the coach has spent countless hours planning and developing plays, strategy and drills for the team. After the game is over and you go home to get ready for tomorrow, many coaches are up reviewing film and analyzing the day's game. For the most part, high school coaches are not getting rich on coaching our children, so it is not for the money. Many have families and lose a lot of time away from their families because they're coaching *our* children.

So why do they do it? Because they love the sport. Because they believe they can make a difference in our children's lives... and many do. To this day, my high school dance coach, Mrs. Meyers, is still one of the most important and influential people in my life.

Although many coaches make it appear easy, coaching high school sports is an incredibly demanding job. In addition to their regular teaching duties, in order to coach our children they're working additional hours, sometimes more than 15 to 20 per week. While they no doubt love of the sport they're coaching, and while the individual high schools and students benefit from their talents and time, adequate compensation remains a struggle for many high schools.

At the football banquet for my son, the head coach, jokingly said that his wife calculated how much he makes, and it adds up to approximately seven cents per hour. How many of us would be willing to work for seven cents per hour? Yet it is done, by a countless number of high school coaches across the country.

THE CHAIN OF COMMUNICATION

High schools, like all organizations, have an established chain of communication. In order for the school to function, and in order to give everyone accountability for their actions, this chain of communication is essential to the daily operations of the school. If you have a problem or concern with your daughter's team or coach, speak with the coach. Many issues can be resolved by talking directly. Even if it cannot be resolved to your liking, at least you will have an answer; and you will have given the clear message to the coach that your child has an involved mom.

If you choose to go directly to the principal, don't be surprised if they ask you if you if you have spoken with the coach or athletic director!

Within a high school here is the order of communication you should probably follow if you have an issue:

<u>After-school sports-related issues</u>
- Coach & athletic trainer (depending on the situation)
- Athletic director
- Principal

<u>Academic-related issues</u>

• Teachers

• Department head or vice principal

• Principal

LESSONS YOUR CHILD *CAN LIVE* WITH

Lesson VI — Observe the chain of communication

Learning how the chain of communication or the chain of command works is a lesson our children will use throughout the rest of their lives. This goes hand-in-hand with respect for authority, which has nothing to do with liking a person.

Our children know who is in charge at their school; and without much thought they go to the correct person for assistance. If you are unsure of whom you should speak with at your child's school, just ask them.

Although the chain of command may have started with the military, most organizations, from corporate businesses, to churches, to hospitals, to educational institutions, have an established chain of communication/command that's essential for effective management and organization.

The majority of high school coaches are fair and truly only want what is best for our children. However, there are those who want to "win" at all costs, and frequently that cost is our children. It is up to you to discern which type of coach your child has. I've heard numerous accounts of students not disclosing pain, illness, or injury to the coach in fear of being yelled at or embarrassed.

We need to let our children know and understand that the day after high school graduation, high school sports will end. Their life is greater than those four years; those four years are supposed to prepare them for the next phase in their life. If they leave it all on the court, track or field in high school, what is left?

Here are a few pointers that can help with how you interface with and communicate with the coach:

- Recognize that the coach has made a huge commitment. In many instances, the coaches are paid very little, if anything. They spend countless hours planning and working with the team.
- Meet the coach as soon as possible. Don't wait until a game is lost to meet the coach as you complain about the game; or wait until your child in injured.

- Coaches are people, too. Be respectful and thankful. Your actions will reflect how your child behaves toward and thinks about that coach.
- Coaches are open to advice. The problem occurs when the advise given at the wrong time, such as during a game; or during a practice. I have seen a situation where a parent actually walked on the field during practice to tell their son how to do something. This is not only wrong, but can be embarrassing for the player.
- Understand that the coach has a high pressure job with little job security. In order to keep their job, the team must show improvement and win. If a game is lost, the coach takes the brunt of the complaints.

STUDENT-ATHLETES CAN SPEAK UP TOO!

As our sons and daughters prepare for life after high school, it may be difficult for many of us to let go. But now is the time to start. High school is the perfect place to begin to take baby steps towards our children's independence; and so high school sports represent a great venue to help them learn how to speak for themselves.

Give them the opportunity to speak to the coach about a problem or situation. Stay in the wings and follow the issue with them, letting them know that they have your full support, but enforcing their responsibility and growth curve.

When the situation involves adverse conduct or health and injury issues, you should be involved from the beginning. Injuries happen on the field, court, track, and in the weight room. Don't assume that every injury makes it to the athletic trainer. If your child comes home injured, ask them what the athletic trainer said. If they tell you that they didn't see the athletic trainer, and you feel the injury is serious enough that they should have been sent to the athletic trainer, make it your business to speak with the coach. You should wonder why your son or daughter was not sent to the athletic trainer. If your child says you will embarrass them by talking to the coach, just remember the following:

- They will get over it.
- They will realize that your actions are out of your love for them.
- You are speaking to the coach because you care.
- You are MOM.

THE COACH'S JOB

The primary responsibility of the coach is to work with our children in a particular sport and help prepare them for competition. In order for them to do this, they must know the rules of the game. They should also have knowledge about safety, equipment, health, and fitness.

The coach must also be able to determine and recognize talent and skills among their players. In many schools or small communities, the coach doesn't have a wide selection of athletes to choose from, so they must be able to make a team out of the available talent and players that want to play.

As a dance coach, I not only teach the young ladies I work with about dance, I am also teaching them about being young ladies. How they carry themselves as young ladies comes across in how they dance. The coaches of our sons and daughters have a great influence on their development. Mom, you need to be aware of this and watch for negative and positive changes, and address both.

Quite frequently, the high school coach has several administrative responsibilities as well. This can include game schedules, equipment maintenance, and scheduling practice facilities. At my son's school, each student must have a certain number of credits in order to play each year. My son's football coach monitored their grades. Considering that he had over eighty players, this was a tremendous task. His job was to step in and offer assistance to my son and his teammates *before* they failed. Many times he benched a player until their grades improved.

DISCIPLINARY ISSUES

The coach is not there to parent disciplinary problems. That's your job. If the coach tells you that your child is disruptive during practice, you need to handle it. Talk to your child about how their behavior affects the rest of the team and slows down practice. Then follow up with the coach in a few days to see if the behavior has changed. This will let the coach know that they can count on you.

Please remember to always show the coach respect in the presence of your child and other players. If you disrespect the coach, and your child sees this, how can you expect them to behave otherwise.

EDUCATION REQUIREMENTS

For most high schools, a bachelor's degree is required. Some may require the coach be state-certified. Many coaches are also required to have experience playing the sport they're coaching. Usually the head coach must have several years as an assistant coach in order to gain that level of responsibility.

Although I wasn't a teacher, having my bachelor's degree in dance and over eighteen years' of dance experience qualified me to assist with the dance team at my son's high school. Although I didn't have a child on the dance team, it was my love of dance that led me to volunteer my time.

A COACH'S DAY

On a typical day a coach may ...
- teach an academic or physical education class.
- meet with teachers of players whose grades are falling.
- meet with the athletic trainer to discuss injuries and upcoming schedule.
- meet with assistant coaches to review film and strategies.
- meet with team managers (usually students).
- manage the team during practices. If there are varsity, JV, and freshman teams, the coach may find themselves running between each.
- motivate the team.

- check equipment.
- monitor the competition.
- sit up late after practice preparing for the next day.
- meet with teachers, the athletic director, and the principal.
- many experienced coaches mentor younger, new coaches.

If you would like to read more about the high school coach, please visit the National High School Athletics Coaches' Association at hscoaches.org.

EXPECTATIONS

For everyone involved (coaches, parents, and the student athlete) there are different levels of expectations. The following may help in clarifying some of these.

What the coach may expect from the student-athlete

Along with having good, clean fun, there are a few simple things your child's coach may expect from them. Share these with your son or daughter:

- show up for practice and games on time, and dressed properly.
- try their best at practice and games.
- get a good night's rest and eat well.
- refrain from the usage of alcohol, drugs and tobacco.
- protect their image and the image of the team and school.
- don't use profane or vulgar language.
- show respect for their teammates.
- show respect for the coaches and officials.
- respect your opponent.
- show appreciation for the coaches and athletic trainer.
- if a change in the schedule conflicts with work, community service, religion, etc., the student-athlete should inform the coach of the conflict as soon as possible.

What the student-athlete may expect from the coach

It is important that our children understand what to expect from the coach. Share these with your son or daughter:

- clear, established team philosophy.
- respect.

- practice and game schedules.
- a fair chance.
- a well thought-out and planned practice.
- a game plan
- respect toward their parents ... us!

What parents can expect from the coach

- clear, established team philosophy.
- expectations of the student-athlete and team.
- respect toward your child and other teammates.
- to set an example for your child and other teammates.
- team practice and game schedule, including locations and times.
- notification of schedule changes.
- team rules and regulations.
- respect toward us!

What the coach may expect from the parents

- direct communication. Always give the coach a chance to explain or correct an issue first.
- let the coach know if there is a situation that may alter your child's schedule.
- speak with the coach if you have a question

about their philosophy and expectations.

• respect the coaching staff and athletic trainer.

• respect toward all players on the team.

• respect toward the opponent players and
  parents.

• behave appropriately at all games.

• never ask the coach about another child.

A COACH'S PERSPECTIVE

What do coaches think? I wanted to know, so I asked.

Q.   *If you were speaking to a group of freshman moms about what to look forward to in high school sports, what would you tell them? This can include whatever you think is important and what you think will help make your job as a coach easier.*

A.   Before I share my perspective on high school sports with a freshman parent, I would listen to what the parent's expectations are of the journey upon which their child and I'll be embarking. One can learn a lot from listening first. One must remember that although a coach is forming a team, freshman parents basically only want to know what benefit the coach and team will provide for their child. A parent cannot be faulted for this approach, as freshman year is the beginning of the end of high school and the transition into college, and a positive team experience does much more for an individual than just earn trophies.

Once I have met my audience and learned of its expectations, I then gladly explain that I, too, share all or most of these expectations for all team members. I would share my philosophy of "building a team ... not a coach" so that the parents realize that I am not living vicariously through the children but rather finding individual strengths and making them stronger and strengthening the areas that require same.

I would then inform the parents that the road may be rocky at times. Perceptions will be made, personalities will clash, jealousy will rear its ugly head and some will quit instead of face the challenge. Whatever the case may be, I'll still be there when the dust clears, the perceptions are realized as such, and the individual realizes that a team is about individuals working together for one goal ... respecting themselves and each other enough to get the job done!

Q.   *What do you enjoy most about coaching high school sports?*

A.   I truly enjoy participating in the growth of the individuals who make up my teams. The changes in personal growth as well as physical and mental maturity are wonderful. When the members begin to "get it" and "want it" makes them learn how to problem solve, interact, tolerate and reap the benefits earned from this growth.

Q.   *Approximately how many hours per week do you spend on coaching during each season?*

A.   Four to 10 hours per week.

Q.   *What is the most rewarding aspect of coaching high school sports?*

A.   Watching the team flourish, take chances, and learn how to handle defeat, turn it into a positive and come back even stronger.

Q.   *Why do you coach high school sports?*

A.   As an educator, I feel that it is important to provide the opportunity for students to join organizations that will require a different type of discipline; a discipline that will play a role in personal growth and future success. As a coach, I, too, grow and learn how to deal with various personalities and how my actions affect others. To me, coaching is a win-win situation. At times, a coach truly learns what it means to "take one for the team".

Q.   *How does coaching high school sports affect your family (wife, husband, kids)?*

A.   I am childless but my husband understands that I am doing what I truly enjoy.

Q.   *What is the hardest aspect of coaching high   school sports?*

A.   Sometimes it feels like there just isn't enough   time.

8 – THE ATHLETIC TRAINER

If the athlete doesn't reveal all the symptoms,
the diagnosis made by the athletic trainer may be
incorrect –
but the athletic trainer is not incorrect.

First, the athletic trainer is neither a doctor nor the coach; he or she is, however, a medical professional trained to understand the complexities of sports injuries that pertain to several different sports. In order for the athletic trainer to treat a sport, they must understand how the body functions within that sport. They should understand anatomy, physiology, and kinesiology. Even as a dance instructor, I was required to study the aforementioned in college.

The athletic trainer must graduate from a program accredited by the Commission on Accreditation of Athletic Training Education and then pass the Board of Certification exam. Once this is complete, the athletic trainer will apply for a license and be registered in the state they wish to work.

Please don't use the athletic trainer's time by asking them coaching questions. They've absolutely nothing to do with what position your child plays or why your child doesn't play. You should not ask them for their evaluation or opinion of the coach or the coach's ability to coach. If your child feels sick in school, don't tell them to see the athletic trainer; send them to the nurse.

The athletic trainer is hired to work for the school and not one specific coach—they work with all the coaches, but report to the athletic director. On any given day, the athletic trainer may be responsible for over a hundred athletes from various different sports.

It is important that you feel comfortable with the athletic trainer, because they're usually the first to diagnose your child's injury. Just as you make the time to meet your child's teachers and coaches, you should make it a point to meet the athletic trainer. Remember, the coaches can change with each sport, but the athletic trainer usually remains the same. Many high schools also have an assigned team physician. Ask the athletic trainer for their name and office phone number. It will not hurt to have this information in your contact list.

If the athletic trainer at your child's school has been working in your school district for a number of years, they should have a good reputation with the local orthopedic doctors and sports doctors. It is reassuring to hear the doctor commend the athletic trainer that has been taking care of your child. When Miles got hurt in his senior year, all of the orthopedic doctors and sports doctor we took him to knew his athletic trainer and had confidence in her ability.

JOB DESCRIPTION

The National Athletic Trainers' Association has defined the public school athletic trainer's job[16]. Their definition includes the following:

- To provide athletic training services to student-athletes, which means to render emergency care along with and the development of injury prevention programs. They also treat and recommend rehabilitation programs for the student-athlete.
- To maintain appropriate treatment records for all student-athletes.

---

[16] For a complete job description, visit
nata.org/employment/job_descriptions/HighSchool_athletictrainer_2005.pdf

- To be present for all home athletic games and away varsity football games. If there is a conflict between an away varsity football game and a home game, the varsity football event will supersede.
- Maintain accurate records of injuries and treatments.
- Provide the coaches and athletic director with a list of athletes medically eligible to compete under district and state rules and regulations.

If you would like to learn more about athletic trainers and their responsibilities, please visit NATA.org.

Speaking with the Athletic Trainer

Since the majority of their work takes place after academic hours, it is not likely to be easy to locate trainers in the earlier part of the day. But right before a game or during a game isn't the best time to speak with the athletic trainer! They're very busy getting ready for the game, just like the coach, and during the game they must follow the game just like the coach. I have found that the best way for me to communicate with my son's athletic trainer was by either sending her an email or leaving her a phone message. She usually called me back in the middle of her day—around noon. If I message was urgent, I would state that.

If your child gets injured, it's okay for you to speak directly with the athletic trainer. Their opinion does matter. However, you know your child best. If they tell you your child's injury is minor, and you disagree or want a second opinion, don't be afraid to ask more questions or get the second opinion. They will not be offended.

In some cases, your child may not want you to take them to the doctor because they're afraid the doctor will tell them not to practice or play. You will need to make that decision. Your decision should be based upon what is best for your child's health and future. You can however, weigh your decision against what both the athletic trainer and your child says.

Don't take offense when speaking to the athletic trainer if takes them a moment to remember who your child is and what is their injury, especially if you don't have your son or daughter with you. Keeping track of over a hundred athletes is not an easy task.

If you are displeased with the athletic trainer, let them know that. But, more importantly, explain to them why. What happened that caused you to feel the way you do. Before you say they misdiagnosed your child, get all the information. Perhaps your child forgot to tell them something.

When my son got hurt, we went to see four different doctors, and he told his story four different ways. The first doctor made his diagnosis based in part on what my son said, and referred him to the second doctor. By the time we saw doctors three and four, my son was able to fully explain what happened, and what had been happening for weeks leading up to his major injury, which drastically changed the recommendation for physical therapy and future sports activities. Do I fault the first two doctors? No. They could only work with what was told to them.

It is imperative that our children understand that withholding symptoms and pain is not in their best interests, and can ultimately be detrimental to themselves and the team.

A good athletic trainer
is worth their weight in gold!

"LESSONS YOUR CHILD *CAN LIVE* WITH"

Lesson VII — Reveal and share symptoms

If your son or daughter has an injury, advise them that ALL symptoms should be told to the athletic trainer, or doctor.

If they're dizzy, throwing up, think they've a fever or feel sick they should report this as well, AND STOP ALL PHYSICAL ACTIVITY.

Our children must use judgment in determining if they're well enough to participate in practice or a game. We are not always there, so they (our children) must be in tuned to their bodies and speak up for themselves.

Make sure they understand that their decision to play sick or injured affects the entire team.

A chain is only as strong as its weakest link. (1b)
Proverb

1b: It is clearly a literal fact that a chain is only as strong as its weakest link. The conversion of that notion into a figurative phrase was established in the language by the 18th century. Thomas Reid's *Essays on the Intellectual Powers of Man*, 1786, included this line:

"In every chain of reasoning, the evidence of the last conclusion can be no greater than that of the weakest link of the chain, whatever may be the strength of the rest."

High School Medical Forms

Don't complain about the medical forms. The information you put on these forms or omit from these forms can drastically affect the care your child receives. If your child takes medication and you leave it off the forms, you are doing your child a disservice. If something happens and emergency care is required, the medical professionals need to know all medications your child is taking. This list affects the care your child will receive and what medications can be administered during emergency medical care.

I have heard parents ask questions like, "why does the school need to know my child's business?" I'll tell you: because as long as your child is playing high school sports, their medical history is the school's business, and *you should want it to be*. Those forms allow the school to help make sure your child is safe and participating in a sport that will not exacerbate a current medical condition.

9 – TEAMMATES

"...we celebrate individual excellence.
But we remember that throughout the games
history, its greatest players—its champions—
are those who don't just perfect their own game,
but make those around them better.
Who unite one team around one shared goal."17

President Barack Obama
February 13, 2009

One of the best times I've ever had is at the end of the game when I am taking my son and several of his teammates home. I lower the radio and listen. This is how I find out what is really going on.

---

17 *"President Obama on the NFL All-Star Game"* Posted by Ann Kinsey, February 13, 2009. presidentobamaquotes.com/2009/02/february-13-2009-president-obama-quotes.html

They talk amongst themselves about the game, the coaches and other players. They will be uncensored and truthful in their opinions and assessment of things if you melt into the fabric of the car, and just let them talk.

When they ask my opinion, I give it. If an injury is mentioned, I recommend that they inform their parents. Sometimes they say "it's okay," but I push a little and try to explain that it is important for their parents to know about all injuries, big and small. Between us moms, it's an unspoken code of conduct. *We look out for each other's children.* If my son gets hit hard at a game, there will be a text or Facebook post the next day simply asking me, "How is Miles?"

It is during these rides that I learn which coaches are liked and disliked, respected and disrespected.

I learn who they like on the team and who they feel is not pulling their weight. They're also honest with each other and show no fear in pointing out each other's shortcomings on the field. I enjoy listening to the mutually shared respect they've developed for each other, and how they can agree with the assessments of each other and then say, "man, you're right. I should have tried harder." Now if they could only talk each other into keeping their rooms clean, making the bed, doing the dishes and volunteering to take out the trash!

10 − ...AND THEN THERE'S DAD!

Sometimes known as the other coach ...

If I miss a game, I usually call my husband and ask about the game. Yes, men are from Mars and women are from Venus.[18] This even applies in sports.

My husband's memory of the game is almost play-by-play, with his opinion interjected along the way. However, what I want to know first and foremost is, "how hard did my son get hit?" (football) or "how far did he throw?" (shot put).

---

[18] *"Men are from Mars, Women are from Venus"* is the title of the book by John Gray (published in May 1992 by Harper Collins)

WHAT ABOUT DAD

Sometimes keeping Dad under control is one of the hardest aspects of the game. He means well and only wants his children to be the best they can be: the leading scorer on the basketball team, the fastest runner on the track team, the best running-back on the football team, and the list goes on. In his zeal to make sure his son or daughter gets to the top of "their" game, he sometimes forgets that he is not the coach. Sometimes we sit with them, sometimes it is best if we just sit amongst ourselves—the moms—and let the dads do their own thing.

In my four years of attending football games, I have never heard a dad wonder if his son ate lunch, or did his homework. I am sure they care about this, but at that moment in time, at the football game, this is far from their minds. On the other hand, several of us moms are wondering about these very things to each other. I even have a friend who packs fried chicken in her purse ... just in case.

Many dads, my husband included, get so involved in the game that they actually get angry and agitated and go home stressed. There are plenty of moms who behave like this at the game. I enjoy listening to them and observing their energy. But win or lose, I enjoy the game, can follow the game, and go home after the game without any stress.

When the game is over, the dads continue to analyze the game. Win, and the dads had a great time! Lose, not so great. Us moms simply tell our sons that they had a great game – win or lose; then proceed to find out if they're hungry and have homework.

"Franco is pretty smart but Franco is a child, and when it comes to the day of the contest, I am his father. He comes to me for advices. And you know, it's not that hard for me to give him, the wrong advices."
Arnold Schwarzenegger

When they lose, some dads want to tell the coach what plays they should or should not have ran, or worse, they proceed to tell their sons what they did or didn't do, sometimes to the embarrassment of their son. Chances are their son will be upset over the loss already. They don't need to add fuel to this fire. This is also not good for the team or the coach to witness. Not to mention us moms, who now have to work at calming down a tired, hungry, upset football player.

11 – HEALTH & NUTRITION
Fuel for the mind, body, and soul!

In all sports, particularly those of the contact nature, there is a force beyond us that takes over our children as they strive to be the best ... to win. Send your child out in as healthy a state as possible and with God as their armor. This means feeding them or making sure they've money or access to enough food to fuel their body and mind.

During football and track season, my son eats approximately four full meals a day, excluding breakfast. For breakfast he prefers a small meal, perhaps a breakfast sandwich or breakfast bar and a drink. Thankfully, he eats a large dinner and therefore is not usually hungry when he wakes. He has learned that if he is hungry in the morning, it not only affects him during sports later that day, but drains him during school hours.

Don't assume that the school will provide a snack or water. Although most, if not all, provide water, you should still send your child with their own supply. In the middle of the summer when it is very hot, send your child to soccer or football practice with their own sports drink to help replenish their electrolytes. Ask your child how much they're drinking during practice or a game. If you are at the game or practice, watch and see how many times they take a drink. If you think they're not drinking enough, sit with them and explain the importance of drinking water and specific sports drinks.

NUTRITIONAL NEEDS FOR THE STUDENT-ATHLETE

As your son or daughter's physical activities increase with the participation in high school sports, so should their daily food intake. Your son may require as many as 5,000 calories a day when he is playing sports, compared to the 3,000 calories he may eat when he is not. Your athletic daughter would require fewer than the 5000, but still an increase from her normal food intake. By making sure our children eat a balanced diet from all food groups we can help them reach these levels.

<u>Food Groups</u>

- bread, cereal, rice, and pasta
- vegetables
- fruit
- milk, yogurt, and cheese
- meat, poultry, fish, beans, eggs, and nuts
- fats, oils, and sweets

For a complete explanation of each food group visit mccaffreys.com/mccaffkid/foodgroups.html

Teaching them how to pack a healthy snack can show them how hoe to eat properly, not to mention saving money.

EATING BEFORE ATHLETIC ACTIVITY

Before a game, the digestive processes may be slowed due to excitement. To allow for this, it's recommended that athletes eat foods that are easily digested no later than three hours before the big game.

I learned this at a very early age, and to this day I have not been able to eat within two to three hours before I dance or do a workout. If I do, I cannot perform to the best of my ability. My stomach cramps and bloats.

My son seems to be okay up to about two hours before a game. However, I noticed that he usually eats the same foods. I once asked him if he got sick during practice from eating two hours before, and he replied, no, he only eats foods that he can digest fast. On his own, he figured this out!

SUPPLEMENTS

Research has shown that supplements present more of a potential problem in our society than steroids, says C. Rogers, a professor of human performance sciences at Adelphi University who specializes in social issues and high school sports.[19] For many athletes, the benefits of taking supplements rarely outweigh the risks. There is little evidence that sports supplements, which represent a 2.7 billion-dollar industry in the U.S., actually enhance athletic performance. Under the Dietary Health and Supplement Education Act of 1994, it is up to the manufacturer to make sure the product is safe. Many

---

[19] "Teens and supplements: An unhealthy mix" article written by Chicago Tribune Staff Writers Julie Deardorff and Jarad S. Hopkins. Found at ctpost.com/health/article/Teens-and-supplements-an-unhealthy-mix-287089.php 12/9/2009

supplements are not recommended for use by persons under the age of eighteen.

Athletes say the pressure to succeed and keep up with peers often drives supplement use. Though whey or soy-based protein supplements are among the most popular products, creatine is frequently used by boys participating in team power sports such as football, wrestling, and hockey.

For our children with underlying health issues, make sure your child's doctor has approved the use of any supplement.

What if your son or daughter wants to take a supplement?

If your son or daughter comes home and tells you about a supplement they would like to take, listen and ask why they feel it is necessary. Then do some research. Read the ingredients. Many supplements are not tested for use under the age of 18, and are not recommended for anyone who has certain ailments and are taking medication.

If you feel you still need more information, call your child's doctor and ask her for her opinion. If your final answer is no, explain why, and explain it in a way that tells the child you don't feel it is a safe supplement for them. When our children turn 18, the game changes. They will be able to purchase and take these supplements without our permission. So the more information we can give them before their eighteenth birthday, the better equipped they will be to make informed decisions.

"LESSONS YOUR CHILD *CAN LIVE* WITH"

**Lesson VIII — Health and nutrition
are vital to success**

As much as we would like to believe it, we don't know everything our children eat or don't eat. If we teach our children about understanding the importance for proper nutrition in order to function in sports and in the classroom, they will be able to make responsible life-sustaining choices.

DRUG ABUSE AND THE IMPORTANCE OF TESTING IN TEENS

A survey conducted in 2008 by Monitoring the Future (MTF) states that almost 47 percent of American teens have experimented with illicit drugs before completing high school.

Teens who participate in competitive sports are more inclined to start steroid or drug use in order to help improve their performance. The runner wants to run faster, the softball player wants to hit farther, the football player wants to lift heavier weights, the long jumper wants to jump higher, or the athlete just wants to have a greater capacity or tolerance level.

No matter what the reason, it is against the law for an athlete to take drugs that enhance natural athletic ability. Testing for drug usage is executed at several stages during the athlete's career: from high school to college to the Olympic Games. If caught, the consequences can be life-altering.

Talking to our children about drugs doesn't end when they enter high school. In fact, the conversations should *increase* then. Know your child: if you notice that your child got bigger, faster, or stronger in a short period of time, engage them in a conversation that will tell you how they got there. Don't be afraid to tell them that you are concerned about drugs. That's not the same as accusing them. Ask if someone is giving them vitamins or aspirin. They might not realize that they've been given drugs. Explain the consequences if drug use is discovered.

I heard a story about a school district where the penalty was equal for drug usage in the school as it was out of the school. Make sure your child understands the penalties issued by their school. I can tell you this: if your child is talented enough to possibly be recruited to play sports in college, discovery of drug usage can severely affect this possibility.

FEMALE HEALTH

Many female athletes have an iron deficiency, particularly during menstruation. If you suspect that your daughter has a low-iron blood count, take her to the doctor to be checked. Buying iron supplements over the counter may appear to be a quick fix, but you will not be able to determine if she is getting the amount that her athletic body needs.

Female Athlete Triad

If you have an athletic daughter, you should pay careful attention to her eating habits and weight loss. The female athlete triad involves disordered eating, amenorrhea, and osteoporosis.

Since the athlete's eating doesn't necessarily mean that she is suffering from anorexia nervosa or bulimia nervosa, it is called "disordered eating" (as opposed to "eating disorder"). Disordered eating can easily lead to the other two components of the female athlete triad, amenorrhea and osteoporosis.

Amenorrhea (loss of menses): If your daughter's menstruation has stopped, you should take her to the doctor to be properly evaluated. Telling the doctor that her menses has stopped is not enough information. Make sure you also tell them that she practices soccer six days a week and hardly eats, etc. This important bit of information can help avoid unnecessary tests and possibly wrong diagnosis. I became aware of the Triad several years ago when a friend became concerned that her daughters' menses had stopped. Turns out, her daughter was hardly eating and dancing and doing gymnastics several hours each day five days a week.

Osteoporosis (loss of bone mineral density): The National Osteoporosis Foundation defines osteoporosis as a disease characterized by low bone mass and deterioration of bone tissue, resulting in bone fragility and increased risk of fracture. An amenorrheic athlete can lose five percent of her bone mass in one year, which may increase the risk of fractures. Proper nutrition is necessary for healthy bone growth, which can be compromised due to disordered eating.

If your daughter, your student-athlete, is affected by disordered eating or has other symptoms of the triad, try to work with her by placing the emphasis on her health and nutrition, and not so much on her size or weight.

Over the years, as girls' involvement has increased in high school sports, our daughters have become more confident in their ability and willingness to try new things.

Positive impact of sports on girls

- Sports and physical activity can help improve self-esteem in girls, especially in those who view themselves as too thin or too large. I am witness to this as I watch the girls I work with grow and mature.
- Being involved in sports and regular physical activity helps girls develop strength and endurance, which leads to the ability to manage their weight more effectively. Last year, I was working with a group of high school students

who thought that they were in better shape than me because they were teenagers, and I was "so old." Did I prove them wrong, and were they ever shocked at how out-of-shape they were!

• When a young woman is involved in sports, she has given herself another reason to be happy. She feels a part of something big.

The athlete's body is their instrument.
Taking care of this instrument is critical to both
mental and physical health,
and nothing is more important than the physical
and mental health of our children ...
of our student-athletes.

12 – INJURIES

The other cost to playing high school sports ... any sport!

The cost of a major injury during a high school sport can make a difference in our children's future lifestyles. However, the reality is that injuries happen when sports are played. Count your blessings if your child plays four years of high school sports without an injury. Although my son's injuries have altered his life plans, I count my blessings, knowing that it could have been worse.

Playing injured and possibly developing a greater injury is a situation that can be avoided. We are our children's biggest fans and we must request medical care when we feel it is necessary, which may from time to time conflict with the coach's need to have them playing.

Remember that in just four short years, our children will not need our permission to play any sports. There will be no permission slips coming home from college. If we allow our children to play injured without medical attention now, this will continue through college and the rest of their lives ... trickling down to *their* children. However, if we show them now that getting medical care is for their best interest and doesn't always result in being told not to play, they will hopefully remember to do the same in the future.

I am all for the team, I am all for my son being "tough" on the field, but at the high school level, our children's health should still be a priority. They can play with some injuries, but with many they cannot and should not.

*I enjoyed high school football games,
but the fear of serious injury
lay in my heart each time my son took the field.*

When I talk with other mothers, this is their major concern as well. I have several friends who will not permit their sons to play football for this very reason. Football, like boxing, is all about contact. There is contact between at least two players every time the ball is snapped or kicked.

There can be a price to playing high school sports. That price is the possibility of injury. Contact sports such as football and wrestling have the highest injury rate, although the overall rate of *severe* injuries is not high.

What is an injury worth to you and your child? I recently heard the story of a high school football player who hurt his hand. The doctors informed his parents that surgery was required and that, without surgery, their son's hand would be permanently deformed. The injury happened right in the middle of the football season. If he had the surgery he would be out for the rest of the season. Staying in the game was more important than a deformed hand, so the student-athlete opted not to have the surgery and his parents agreed. Go figure!

No sport is played without some injuries, so if your child plays high school sports you should be prepared for this possibility.

It is easy for us to see and monitor the injuries sustained by professional athletes, because they're broadcast on the news and media. What we fail to realize is that teenage athletes are injured just as much. It's sometimes difficult to determine when an injury is serious enough to take your child to the doctor, which is why it's important that you listen to your child's complaints about injuries and pain.

When Miles complained that his hip hurt, we had him looked at by the athletic trainer. However, after a few weeks of stretching and icing during which it didn't get better, we took him to the doctor. He had injured his growth plate. This type of injury happens in many contact sports. The orthopedic expert explained that this was an injury that needed to be healed before Miles could go back to football. The doctor further explained that for some sports, his return would be sooner, but as a 240-pound defensive lineman, who needed to push up and off his legs and through his hips, this needed to be one hundred percent healed in order to avoid additional injuries.

Student-athletes playing contact sports have a greater chance than others of sustaining a serious injury. An injury is classified as severe if the athlete misses more than twenty-one days of sports activity. A study by researchers from Ohio State University College of Medicine and the Center for Injury Research and Policy in the Research Institute at Nationwide Children's Hospital, both in Columbus, Ohio, took the data collected from the academic years 2005 through 2007 in 100 high schools nationwide from nine sports revealed that 57percent of all injuries resulted in medical disqualification for the rest of the season. [20]

---

[20] *"All High School Sports Injuries are not created equal"* by Jeannie Stein September 3, 2009 http://latimesblogs.latimes.com/booster_shots/2009/09/as-the-kids-head-back-to-school-theyll-also-head-back-to-team-sports-so-brace-yourselves-moms-and-dads-for-the-inevitable.html

In the September issue of the *American Journal of Sports Medicine*, researchers in the Center for Injury Research and Policy (CIRP) of the Research Institute at Nationwide Children's Hospital state that males experienced a higher rate of severe injuries over females. Twenty-nine percent of severe injuries are to the knees; while twelve percent of the injuries are sustained to the ankle, explained the study's co-author Christy Collins, CIRP research associate at Nationwide Children's Hospital. [21]

BREAKDOWN OF INJURIES[22]

Severe and Common Injury Diagnosis
- Fractures 36 percent
- Complete ligament sprains 15 percent
- Incomplete ligament sprains 14 percent

Commonly Fractured Body Sites
- Hand and finger 18 percent
- Ankle 14 percent

21

redorbit.com/news/education/1747238/certain_high_school_athletes_suffer_highest_rate_o
f_severe_injuries/index.html
22

redorbit.com/news/education/1747238/certain_high_school_athletes_suffer_highest_rate_o
f_severe_injuries/index.html

• Wrist 11 percent

What are the top-ranked sports for injuries?

Football has the highest injury rate of all high school sports. In looking at this number, you must remember that there are over one million high-schoolers playing football annually. Next is wrestling, with girls' basketball and soccer following third and fourth. Boys tend to have a higher injury rate than girls. However, in basketball, girls have a higher injury rate than do boys.

In the article "2010 Fitness Trends," the American College Sports of Medicine publishes fitness trends for 2010. Strength training is number one! Pilates comes in at number nine and yoga at number 14. High school athletes are incorporating training into their off-season in order to stay in top shape for their sports.

Expanded practices, off-season and on, including combines and summer camps have added to the noticed increase in student injuries. The Center for Disease Control's *High School Sports Related Injury Surveillance Study* confirmed these negative trends: "High school athletes account for an estimated two million injuries, 500,000 doctor visits, and 30,000 hospitalizations annually."[23]

ONE OF THE MOST SERIOUS INJURIES – A CONCUSSION

A concussion is a *brain injury*. Take it seriously. Many people tend to think that a person has to pass out in order to have a concussion, but that's far from the truth. My son got two concussions playing football. He was able to walk and talk and he never lost consciousness. In fact, he didn't realize he had the first concussion until after the second one was diagnosed!

The signs of a concussion are not easy to recognize. Because of this, many players continue to play, which puts them and their teammates at serious risk.

Concussions account for almost 10 percent of sports injuries, and are the most common type of brain injury. "More than 1.2 million teenagers play high school football every fall, and hundreds are seriously injured by concussions and other brain trauma. About 400,000 concussions occurred in high

---

[23] http://high school-culture.suite101.com/article.cfm/high_school_sports#ixzz0WZyuksUJ - Article by Michael Streich

school athletics during the 2008-2009 school year—more in football than in any other sport," says the *Times*.[24]

My son's doctors gave me a list of symptoms to look for. Here is a list of signs and symptoms that you should be aware of if a concussion is suspected:

- "Seeing stars" and feeling dazed, dizzy, or lightheaded
- Memory loss, such as trouble remembering things that happened right before and after the injury
- Nausea or vomiting
- Headaches
- Blurred vision and sensitivity to light
- Slurred speech or saying things that don't make sense
- Difficulty concentrating, thinking, or making decisions
- Difficulty with coordination or balance (such as being unable to catch a ball (or other easy tasks)
- Feeling anxious or irritable for no apparent reason
- Feeling overly tired

---

[24] http://trueslant.com/caitlinkelly/2009/10/30/400000-high school-football-players-got-concussions-this-year-what-exactly-is-the-point/ Article by Caitlin Kelly

Concussions are seen among soccer and baseball players as well, and they don't stop there. We've heard of cases where a basketball player diving for a ball got kneed in the head, or a baseball player getting "beaned" by a fastball.

There was a story in the news about a 16-year-old girl in New Jersey who had to give up basketball because she suffered multiple concussions. Not only did she give up basketball, but her quality of life and ability to function in school were both drastically affected.

Growing concern over head injuries has required the NFL to explain to the U.S. Congress its treatment of head injuries with regard to retired players and give evidence of long-term effects. Many high school athletes and their coaches are modeling their behavior according to the NFL.

The NFL has been asked to take a look at procedures as they pertain to head injuries. In doing this, the organization released new, stricter guidelines for dealing with players who suffer from head injuries/concussions. If they're taking a closer look at what they're doing, then so should we, Mom, be making sure our children receive proper medical care when a head injury occurs.

The University of Michigan released a study noting that the rate of dementia symptoms for former football players over age 50 was five times the national average, and for players between 30 and 49 it was 19 times higher than the average.[25]

On March 4, 2010, the National Federation of State High School Associations (NFHS) released a press release regarding concussions. Effective in the 2010 high school football season, any player who shows signs, symptoms, or behaviors associated with a concussion must be removed from the game and shall not return to play until cleared by an appropriate health-care professional. [26]

Is a college scholarship worth the dangers of a concussion? Only you and your son or daughter can answer this. Mom, here is a small bit of reality. If your child is eighteen years old and has the opportunity to play college sports, you cannot stop it! So what do you do? You educate your children about injuries and concussions. At least they will have the information and can make an informed decision.

Not that any of us will sleep any better ...

---

[25] mlive.com/sports/grand-rapids/index.ssf/2009/12/concussion_trend_changing_how.html. Article by Greg Johnson.
[26] nfhs.org/content.aspx?id=3853 *Concussion Rule Revised, Strengthened in High School Football – Press Release 3/4/10*

Should your child play high school sports?

After reading all this information about injuries, should you still allow your child to play high school sports? "Data such as this shouldn't deter parents from allowing their children to play sports," says Dawn Comstock, assistant professor of pediatrics at Ohio State University College of Medicine. "We have an epidemic of obesity in this country, and most kids today get the majority of their physical activity from organized sports. We should focus on making sports as safe as possible so kids can incorporate them as part of a healthy lifestyle."

The study can be found in the September 2009 issue of the *American Journal of Sports Medicine*.

Mental Health

Although not a physical injury, mental health problems, if not treated, can quickly become physical problems. All of our children are different and handle the stress of sports, the game, the team, the coach, homework, etc., differently. Know your child, so that you can spot changes in their behavior before it becomes a problem. Children can be depressed and not know they're depressed, and if we're not tuned in to our children, we won't know, either.

A few years ago, I was talking to the mother of one of my son's friends. She casually mentioned that she would be glad when the season was over. I asked her why. She answered, still casually, that all her son did was stay in his room after he came home from practice or a game. He wouldn't talk and barely ate. Guess what? He was depressed!

13 – ACADEMICS

The reason our children are in high school!

In his article, *The Downside of Athletic Programs Destroys Academic Balance,* Michael Streih writes that "high school athletic programs should be treated as a necessary and vital part of the education process, but not at the expense of academic standards and expectations."[27] I could not agree more.

What are your priorities?
Academics vs. sports

---

[27] http://high school-culture.suite101.com/article.cfm/high_school_sports

How does a child find the balance between sports and academics? There were times when my son didn't get home from a game until after ten o'clock in the evening. This means that he left the house at 6:45 am and didn't get back home until over sixteen hours later.

How was he expected to keep up with schoolwork? But he was. He was also required to attend practices or meets on the weekends. My son quickly had to figure out how to get it all done. It took a while, but eventually he found his rhythm.

Remember when looking at professional athletes that they're paid, and they're paid to entertain us. Our high school student-athletes play sports to enhance their high school experience. We need to keep our kids grounded in this reality, always emphasizing that **the purpose of high school is to get an education**.

In an interview that *Wall Street Journal* senior economics writer Stephen Moore conducted with Mayor Dave Bing of Detroit, it's evident that athletes can go further than the court. After playing in the NBA for over 10 years, Dave Bing was in business for 29 years before taking on the role of mayor. Mr. Bing noted that he felt passionately about the value of sports in the lives of young people. Before he became mayor, he donated and helped raise money to keep high school sports programs in Detroit.[28]

"I think sports are critical," he says. "I don't care whether it's in the inner city or not, if the only thing that we prepare young folks today for is classroom activities they lose a lot. There's so much you can learn in sports that you don't learn from academics. Understanding how to get along and communicate with people. Being part of a team. Sports gives you a sense of what it's like to win, and how you handle losing and setbacks, which life is full of." [29]

There is some evidence suggesting that athletes possess stronger leadership skills than non-athletes. I cannot say for sure, but as a mom, coach, and athlete, I can say it teaches you how to work within a team—and how to emerge from that team as an individual.

Growing up in the projects in the Bronx, I was fortunate to belong to an organization called The Boys' Athletic League. This organization was not only my first

---

[28]
http://online.wsj.com/article/SB10001424052748703558004574581650636077732.
html- *Can Detroit Be Saved?* Article by Stephen Moore
[29]
http://online.wsj.com/article/SB10001424052748703558004574581650636077732.
html -*Can Detroit Be Saved?* Article by Stephen Moore

employer, (at age 12 I was teaching dance to little kids!), but it sponsored athletic teams, tournaments, and events. Whenever possible, staff brought in pro athletes to talk to us, and each summer we visited the New York Jets' training camp. I learned to play basketball, softball, and handball, started dancing, and learned how to box. It was through athletics, that I (and many of my friends) got the opportunity to attend college. The Boys' Athletic League taught us that a combination of academic excellence mixed with sports talent made a path for a great future and further education. Between the confidence instilled in my by my high school coaches and the exposure gained from this organization, I was ready and prepared for college.

Many college coaches will not even consider a student's athletic ability if his or her grades are not up to par. Before Miles' injury, and when we were visiting colleges, every coach asked about his grades. Academics and sports go hand in hand in order to help develop our children into educated responsible adults.

DOCTORING GRADES

In most high schools, the teacher plays an important role along with the coach. No teacher wants to see a student fail, but being an athlete should not be the teacher's reason for passing a student.

Although I am directly unfamiliar with anyone who has benefited from doctored grades, my research tells me that it does happen. Here are four different scenarios:

- Fraudulent transcripts are sent to colleges which misrepresent the students' grades. When this happens, the cumulative grade point average of the student-athlete is raised. Afterward, the grades are changed back.
- Original permanent high school records are lost.
- Student-athletes' grades are changed without supporting documentation.
- Student athletes graduate without fulfilling necessary graduation requirements.

It may appear that the student-athlete is benefiting from these doctored grades, but they're not. In the end, they will suffer, because aside from playing sports in college, the student-athlete must also maintain a certain grade point average set by the individual school.

One of the responsibilities of high school is to prepare our children for college (both sports *and* academics), and not to send them into the world falsely prepared. If the above infractions are discovered, the school administration would mostly be reprimanded, perhaps even fired, but in the end it will be your child that suffers most. Quite possibly, the college will rescind its offer, which will leave your child where?

By the time your son or daughter is ready to send out their college applications, you should know what their GPA is. Match it to qualifying schools. You also have the right to request a copy of the transcript sent to colleges. If you suspect that something is incorrect or suspect, check. Better to correct it now than when your child has been accepted and committed.

NCAA STUDENT-ATHLETES GRADUATION RATE

According to the NCAA, college graduation rates have hit an all-time high since the numbers were first tracked eight years ago. Seventy-nine percent of all Division I athletes who entered college from 1999 to 2002 graduated within six years of enrolling. However, as an individual sport, men's basketball and football still lag behind at 64 percent and 67 percent respectively.[30]

Sport-by-Sport Graduation Success Rates

A report issued by the NCAA in November of 2009 states that the overall graduation success rate for all NCAA athletes who entered college from 1999 to 2002 is 79 percent. The overall federal rate for athletes is 64 percent. (To read the full news report, visit ncaa.org.)

---

[30] *"Athletes' Graduation Rates Hit Another High, NCAA Says"* Article by Libby Sander -- http://chronicle.com/article/Athletes-Graduation-Rates-Hit/49202/

14 – GAME DAY

This is what they practice for!
This is what you pay for!

Countless hours of time. Bruised and battered bodies from football, swollen fingers from bowling, twisted ankles from cheerleading, tired legs from track and field, many worn shoes from golf, tired muscles from weightlifting, broken strings from tennis and lacrosse, dulled blades from ice hockey, along with an endless supply of sports drinks leads up to this one moment in time. Game day!

In my home, the energy is slightly higher on game day, including mine. Miles is usually a little subdued, anxious and nervous all at once. I think it helps when he has school first. He gets to see that his teammates are feeling the same.

I carefully monitor my activities at work in order to ensure that I leave in plenty of time to travel to the game. Miles' dad rushes home from his job, walks the dog, then meets me at the game. As I approach the place where I want to sit, I pass several other moms. We are excited to see each other and give each a nod for being there. The silent "salute" for a job well done. You made it to the game ... our sons' football game!

We talk briefly about our boys during half time ... a little about the game. The dads seem to have the corner on that. As we went from freshman moms to senior moms, our conversations grew from general childcare, food, school, and sports to include girlfriends, working after school, driving, and college, and somehow we always manage to fit it all into the twelve minutes allotted. We live the evolution of our children from the stands at the football games. It was a comfort to see that we were all experiencing the same things at the same time.

I remember the first football game, four years ago, when my son was a freshman and went to the locker room for half-time. Several of us moms wondered if those twelve minutes were going to be enough to give our tired sons a rest. Now as a senior mom, it's "why does half-time have to be so long? They don't need to rest too long, their bodies will get cold." How we change with our children!

Spring track was a little different. I didn't get to sit as much. I walked from venue to venue and enjoyed watching my son and my friends' children compete. After a while, I usually found a spot near the track and enjoyed the rest of the meet from there. Several hours later, I'd get in my car and drive to school to pick him up.

Well, that was before he and his friends were driving! This year, I'll just go home. He will most likely get something to eat with his teammates and then come home.

As I write this, I realize that Miles is in the middle of winter track. Next will be spring track and then it's over for high school sports. He's begun to enjoy a year of "lasts." Not just the last football game, or last throw of the shot put, but the last film viewing, the last workout, his last varsity ceremony and banquet.

"What will you do with your newfound time when Miles leaves for college?" a friend asked me the other day. So I ask you, if your child is a senior, what will *you* do with *your* newfound time? Plan it carefully.

They will be home from college in four short years! Me, I want to travel.

Enjoy each game like it is your last, because the four years of high school go by quickly!

15 – SOCIAL MEDIA

Socializing from the comfort of one's bedroom!

Social media is media designed to be shared through social interaction, created by using various publishing techniques.

The usage of social media is believed to be a major factor in the idea that we are living in the Attention Age.[31]

COMMON FORMS OF SOCIAL MEDIA[32]

---

[31] The Attention Age is marked by the ability of individuals to create and consume information instantly and freely as well as share it on the internet using social media. The period is believed to have begun with the emergence of social media in the first years of the 21st century. Found at http://en.wikipedia.org/wiki/Attention_Age

- Concepts, slogans, and statements with a high memory-retention quotient, that excites others to repeat.
- Grassroots direct action information dissemination such as public speaking, installations, performance, and demonstrations.
- Electronic media with sharing, syndication, or search algorithm technologies (includes internet and mobile devices).
- Print media designed to be redistributed.

What does this mean for our children? It means that they're social networking ... a lot!

SOCIAL NETWORKING

Our children are social networking daily with their friends. Countless hours are spent sharing photos, poetry, their plans for today and for tomorrow. In fact, they will even communicate with each other this way while in the same room. It also means that they're

---

[32] http://en.wikipedia.org/wiki/Social_media

developing research skills, which can help them later in life with college or employment.

Our athletic high school children looking to play at the next level can use some of this time and these skills to help promote themselves. TAKKLE and beRecruited are two social networks developed specifically for the high school student-athlete.

TAKKLE.com

TAKKLE is a social network for high school sports, developed to help high school student-athletes network. The student-athlete can create their own profile, upload photos and videos, and log their stats. They can also obtain information about opposing teams and rivals.

When they're ready to begin the college search, the student-athlete can send the "TAKKLE Sheet," a one-page snapshot of their stats, to college coaches. They can also invite friends, teammates, coaches, and family to join.

TAKKLE.COM is a partner of National Collegiate Scouting Association. We'll discuss NCSA's services in the next chapter.

beRecruited.com: Connecting High School Athletes & College Coaches

beRecruited is a social network for today's high school student-athletes who are seeking recruitment from colleges and university coaches. beRecruited allows student-athletes to connect and interact with college coaches. The network gives student-athletes the tools to research and build their athletic and academic profiles. The website also provides coaches with searchable database of potential recruits.

NEGATIVE SOCIAL NETWORKING

Teach your children that if their friends can read it, so can school officials, and everyone else. Negative tweets, blogs, Facebook notes, etc., about coaches, teachers, and fellow teammates can be extremely disruptive to the team. Not to mention hurtful in some cases.

Although they may think what they're saying is private or going to be kept among friends, with everyone interacting with everyone else, very little is kept private within a community or high school.

And especially not on the internet. Once it's out there, it's out there forever, a concept that isn't familiar to many young people.

16 – PLAYING AT THE NEXT LEVEL

Be prepared!
As soon as your child indicates that playing in college is a dream, wish, or possibility, the recruiting process begins.
This may even happen before high school.

It may be happening and they're not even aware that it is!

What do you do when your son or daughter says that they want to play sports in college?

First, you shouldn't be surprised. If you have been a part of your child's high school sports career, you already know whether or not they've talent in their chosen sport. In fact, you may have started thinking about this prior to high school.

This is my favorite chapter because, by the time you get here, you have a good understanding of what is happening with your child in high school sports. Moving on to the next level is an anticipated adventure for your family.

One of the most important organizations in the process is the National Collegiate Athletic Association (NCAA).

WHAT DOES THE NCAA DO?[33]

The NCAA serves as the athletics governing body for more than 1,300 colleges, universities, conferences, and organizations. The member colleges and universities develop the rules and guidelines for athletics eligibility and athletics competition for each of three NCAA divisions.

---

[33] For detailed information about the NCAA visit at http://eligibilitycenter.org. NCAA Eligibility Center 2009-10 guide for the College-Bound Student-Athlete. Where Academic and Athletics Success is Your Goal. Page 2. Published by the NCAA.

WHAT IS THE DIFFERENCE BETWEEN DIVISIONS I, II AND III?

Following is a brief description of the differences between the three college sport divisions. I've visited college from all three divisions and listened to several coaches talk about NCAA rules and regulations; but for a more detailed description of the three divisions, visit ncaa.com.

Division I

Division I schools must offer a minimum of seven sports for men and seven for women (or six for men and eight for women). A total of 14 sports must be offered each year. Football bowl subdivision teams must meet a minimum attendance of an average 15,000 people in actual or paid attendance per home game, which must be met once in a rolling two-year period. There are minimum financial and maximum financial aid awards established. This may differ from sport to sport.

Division II

Division II schools must sponsor at least five sports for men and five for women (or four for men and six for women) for a total of 10 sports each year. There are no attendance requirements for football, and there are maximum financial aid awards for each sport.

Division III

Division III schools must offer a minimum of five sports for men and five for women, for a total of 10 sports. There are no financial aid awards related to the athletic ability of the student.

At the beginning of your child's junior year or at the end of the sophomore year, when they're selecting their junior classes, plan to meet with their high school guidance counselor so that he or she is aware of and understands that your son or daughter wants to play at the next level. This is a very important step because there are NCAA course and SAT requirements for both Division I and II schools.

You should also be aware of the requirements set by each college or university your child is applying to. Often individual schools' requirements may be different from those of the NCAA, in which case your son or daughter may need to meet both levels of requirements.

MYTH VERSUS FACTS

The conversation you have with your son or daughter should be based on fact and not myth. There are countless myths about college recruiting. Here are a few that I'd like to share:

Myth – There are an endless number of athletic scholarships available at the college level.
Fact – A fraction of the number of student-athletes playing sports in high school will receive athletic scholarships to NCAA Division I and II schools.

Myth – Your son or daughter will get a full athletic scholarship for four years that will cover all college costs.
Fact – Most college athletic scholarships don't cover 100 percent of college costs.

Myth – The high school coach has the responsibility to help your son or daughter get a college scholarship.
Fact – The high school coach's responsibility to your son or daughter is to coach them in high school. They don't have the responsibility to help your son or daughter get a college scholarship.

Myth – We don't need to get our own footage, we will get it from the coach.

Fact –Remember, the coach's primary purpose is to coach high school sports. He or she may not have the time to pull footage for your child in the middle of the season.

Myth – We have time. My son is just a junior.

Fact – You don't have time, the process has already begun.

Myth – My daughter is Division I material because she is the best player on her team.

Fact – Understand your child's personality. Even though she's an excellent athlete, Division I may not be for her. She may fit better at a Division II or III school. Also, remember that many colleges are recruiting across the country—not just in your hometown!

Myth – All Divisions start making their decisions during the student-athletes senior year.

Fact – Many Division I schools have already made their final decisions before the student-athlete reaches their senior year.

Myth – My child's grades and classes taken in high school don't matter.

Fact – This is far from the truth. Not only do their grades and classes taken matter, but their SAT scores also play a big factor in being accepted into many college sports programs.

There are several aspects of the NCAA process that are critical. Every parent of a prospective college-bound student-athlete should be aware of NCAA rules and regulations. Don't leave it up to your child to figure all this out on their own.

Begin to build their athletic and academic resumes. Keep track of their accolades.

I started reading about NCAA regulations at the end of my son's sophomore year. It began with the selection of his junior-year classes. Being familiar with this can help you and your son or daughter figure out which level of college play is best for them.

My son chose to attend a Division II school. Although he cannot play football, we still made sure that he was compliant with the NCAA rules and regulations for that division. Who knows, he might decide to try out for a different sport once he gets there!

Over 30 sports are sponsored by the NCAA. For a complete listing of these sports, read the *NCAA Eligibility Center 2009-10 Guide for the College-Bound Student-Athlete: Where Academic and Athletics Success is Your Goal.*

RECRUITING TERMS[34]

As noted earlier, student-athletes, their families, and college coaches must follow certain rules and regulations set by the NCAA. There are several recruiting terms that govern these rules, and you and your son or daughter should be familiar with them.

Having completed several months of recruiting with my son, and meeting with a number of college coaches and admissions personnel, the following 10 terms became second nature to us. (For a complete list and full details of these terms, read the *NCAA Eligibility Center Guide for the College-Bound Student-Athlete.*)

---

[34] NCAA Eligibility Center 2009-10 Guide for the College-Bound Student-Athlete. Where Academic and Athletics Success is Your Goal. Page 18. Published by the NCAA.

Contact: Any face-to-face contact between a college coach and your child, or you, which happens away from the college campus and the coach says more than a simple hello.

Contact Period: Contact with your son or daughter and/or you on or off the college's campus is permitted. The coach may also visit their high school and observe them playing. The coach may write and telephone your child during this period.

Dead period: Only written or telephone contact is permitted.

Evaluation: An evaluation is when a coach evaluates your child's academic or athletic ability. This can include visiting their high school or watching them practice or compete.

Official Visit: If the college pays for the visit, it is an official visit. Here are some of the expenses the college may pay for:

- Your transportation to and from the college.
- Room and meals while you are visiting the college. Limited to three per day.
- Three complimentary tickets to a home game.

Before your son or daughter can go on an official visit, they will have to provide the college with a copy of their high school transcript (Division I only) and SAT, ACT or PLAN score and register with the eligibility center. We will discuss the official visit in greater detail later in this chapter.

Prospective Student-Athlete: Once the ninth-grade begins your son or daughter becomes a "prospective student-athlete." This can happen sooner if a college gives them any financial aid or other benefits that the college doesn't normally provide to students.

Unofficial Visit: If you visit a college and you pay for it, it is an unofficial visit. The college may however offer you three complimentary tickets to a home game.

Verbal Commitment: This phrase is used to describe a future college student-athlete's commitment to a school before they sign a National Letter of Intent. This "commitment" is not binding on either the college or student-athlete.

Recruiting Calendars: To see recruiting calendars for all sports go to NCAA.org.

National Letter of Intent: The National Letter of Intent (NLI) is administered by the Eligibility Center. The letter is an official agreement for one academic year only.

COLLEGE RECRUITING - WHAT PARENTS NEED TO KNOW AND DO

The information in this section, unless otherwise noted, is provided by courtesy of the National Collegiate Scouting Association (NCSA) - ncsasports.org.

"LESSONS YOUR CHILD *CAN LIVE* WITH"

Lesson IX — Plan ahead

Teaching our children that planning is a critical skill to success is very important.

As you plan financially for their college career, you should also plan the recruitment process.

Making your child a part of this plan will teach them valuable lessons for life. It will also give them a sense of responsibility for their future.

Here are four questions you should ask:

1. How competitive are college sports?
2. What does my child need in order to gain a competitive advantage over their peers?
3. How much time and money can I–the parent– expect to spend?
4. What activities should we invest in?

How competitive is it to play sports in college?

The numbers are staggering, yet it's important for you to understand how they correlate to the big picture.

Over 500,000 high school boys played basketball in 2008-09. There are approximately 1730 college basketball programs, including junior college, NAIA, NCAA D1, D2, and D3. Each college has an average of twelve players on their roster. Only a fraction of the 500,000 plus basketball players will have the qualifications, both athletically and academically to be eligible to play at the college level.

Even with this, each player who wants to play at the next level will be competing with approximately five other kids. They will have about a 17 percent to 25 percent chance to play depending upon the sport. So the question for us parents is, "what will give our children the competitive advantage to be one of the chosen and actually get to play and get college funded?

What do parents need to do to give their son or daughter a competitive advantage?

The student-athlete should be competing at the highest level possible in their sport. In many cases this will mean going beyond high school.

Every sport has outside programs. There are camps, combines, travel teams, all-star programs, elite programs, etc. Most of these outside activities cost money. As I pointed out earlier, there is a cost for our children to play sports and this cost continues here. Even the most elite athletes have personal trainers to help get the edge over the other elite athletes.

Don't sit back and think your child will be discovered because they're the best at their high school – invest in your child.

So what should your budget be to get your child recruited? What is the best way to invest your money?

How much of an investment needs to be made in time and scarce resources?

There are three areas that you should invest in to help make sure that your child is in the best position to be recruited:

- On the athletic side you will probably spend anywhere from $1,000 to $5,000 per year. More if your child plays sports outside of high school.
- On the academic side, you'll want to keep track of your child's grades in school. If they need help, get them the help. If their high school doesn't offer SAT or ACT preparatory classes, you may need to invest in this as well.
- Recruiting. For the most part, the recruiting budget for most colleges is rather small. They cannot afford to travel across the USA and discover your child. You have to devote time and funds to marketing your child. Yes, I said it ... marketing your child!

If over four years of high school you spend $4,000 to $20,000 on athletic development—and additional money on academic development—so that your child can qualify for a college athletic scholarship, what is the payoff for your investment? Don't blink at the $20,000. Take a moment and list all of your expenses today, starting with their freshman year of high school. How far are you from this $20,000 mark? If your child is a senior, not far, I bet, if your child has attended camps, combines, elite events, and played on teams outside of high school. Use the list in chapter five as a starting point to help you track your expenses.

Marketing your son or daughter is an important skill that Keith Babb, author of the article series *What Parents Need To Do,* says 99 percent of parents don't know how to do.

This was my favorite part of my son's high school career! As a marketing professional, I enjoyed promoting my most precious of all products—my son. I approached his prospective college career as another product or brand ... the Miles Winfrey brand. I didn't market him solely as an athlete; I also marketed him as a student, an asset for the college. I think it is important to have a general understanding of this, because if your child, like mine, finds him or herself in a position where they can no longer play sports, you haven't lost time in the college recruiting process.

I established a budget, timeline, and meeting schedule. We had college night at least twice a month during his junior and senior years until he made a decision. Once he made the decision, our time was spent on planning for college. We joined the NCSA family in his junior year. The information received from NCSA was invaluable. By the time Miles was starting his senior year in high school he was ready for the process. His classes were in line with NCAA. His SAT scores were within their guidelines. In fact, we added additional classes in his senior year that were on their core list, just to be sure.

He attended Schuman's National Underclassmen Combine[35] where he not only had his skills certified, but had a video produced as well that we placed online for viewing by college coaches. (Many contacts were made through this video!) It was an enjoyable experience for Miles. During the combine, he was followed by an assigned cameraman who was able to capture him at his

---

[35] The National Underclassmen Combine gives high school football players the opportunity to showcase their abilities and gain exposure with colleges from Divisions I, II and III. The combine includes the 40-yard dash, shuttle run, vertical jump, broad jump and bench press tests. There are individual workout sessions for each football position and one-on-one and three-on-three competitions. For more information visit http://nationalunderclassmen.com.

best. A new email account was set up for college usage only.

The best part of this was that he was an active participant, to the point where when we visited colleges, I was able to walk away or sit quietly and let him speak with college coaches and admissions personnel. He knew what was going on.

This was critical because it is his life, not mine. For me, it was like having a part-time job; but for him, it was preparation for the next phase of his life. Most importantly, he knew that even with all our efforts, there was no guarantee that he would get recruited or even play at the college level. But he wouldn't be able to say that we didn't try.

I must add here that, although I am a marketing professional, it never occurred to me to "market" my son until I got involved with NCSA.

All of our efforts no longer benefit my son, but what I learned I am sharing with you and hopefully it will benefit your son or daughter.

NCSA has devoted a great deal of time and effort to educate student-athletes and us (the parents) on marketing our children. Some parents do all of this on their own. It is doable, but not without an extreme commitment. If you are a busy mom, like me, hiring a professional recruiter may be the best way for you and your family.

What activities should you invest in?

In order for you to properly market your son or daughter, there are several things that need to be done:

1. Formally evaluate your son or daughter's skills/talents, so that you can target the right college programs. Division I and II are not for everyone. Some would do much better at the Division III level.

2. Prepare and post an online resume. Bring this resume with you on all college visits.

3. Have a highlight and/or skills video prepared. The skills video is okay for an introduction if your child doesn't have a highlight video, but most coaches will also ask for a highlight video.

4. Make contact with as many college coaches as possible. Try to reach at least 100 coaches. This may seem like a lot but it isn't. This will take a lot of time and effort.

5. Help your child consider all options. Don't rule out Division III and only look at Divisions I and II. You should help your child match the school, the division and majors offered to their preferences.

College coaches get inundated with resumes, emails, and DVDs. You have to work with your child so that they stand out. College coaches rely on trusted sources and verified information. This is where a professional recruiter or combines comes in for verifying skills.

Visiting colleges and meeting coaches is another way to help your child get their name out there. I remember my son's first contact with a college coach. As we approached the coach, I handed him the resume, stepped aside, and told him I would wait for him.

Although I'd prepared him for this by doing mock sessions, the look on his face told me he was terrified; but off he went—and he survived. I knew he would. After about 10 minutes, the coach and my son looked in my direction and waved me over. I was now being invited into the conversation.

I learned this from NCSA. I cannot speak for my son. The coach is not interested in me … yet. By the time my son met with the fifth coach, he was an old pro. He knew how to collect business cards. He knew that he needed to write the coach a short thank-you note. If the coach asked for something, he either sent it or mentioned it in his note to the coach.

Each time my son sent out his video—either skills or footage—he included his resume and a short typed and signed letter. Presentation goes a long way. A video in an empty envelope goes to the bottom of the pile. A video with a well-written note may get put at the top of the pile.

When it came time to send out college applications, his resume was once again included. If he filed online, the resume was sent under separate cover. His resume included his picture in the upper right-hand corner. Next to the picture was a quote from the local newspaper about him. (I said I was a marketing manager, didn't I?) When his application was received, admissions would automatically know that they had a prospective student-athlete.

We had one situation in which the school returned his application fee, saying the football coach had waived the fee for him. And several schools called to say they were impressed with his application packet. Just as when you're looking for a job, presentation goes a long way.

RECRUITING HELP

If you decide to hire a professional recruiter or recruiting company, here is a list of things you may want to find out about them:

- Are they an individual, franchise, or corporation? How long have they been in business? You are looking for someone who is known in the college coaching community.
- How are the student-athletes marketed to the college coaches? Will you be able to track which college coaches reviewed your child's resume and video?
- What is the organization's relationship with college coaches?

- Do college coaches reach out to them and request student-athlete information?

- Are they considered a leader in the recruiting industry?
- Who are the partners of the recruiting company?
- What type of customer service is available?
- Do they offer financial aid advice and parent coaching?
- How will your child be able to determine what college coaches are truly interested in them?
- Will you get a refund if your child suffers a career-ending injury and cannot play in college?
- Make sure they present you with a clear contract spelling out everything you will receive. You don't want any hidden costs.

Being a part of our children's life decisions is one of our greatest rewards. Going from high school to college for the student-athlete is a very trying process. It can be scary at times for them. The fact that you have read this far means that your child is very lucky to have you as a parent.

Social Media in College Recruiting

The NCAA has applied the rules they already had in place for social media recruiting to Twitter and Facebook. Coaches are forbidden to speak about recruits, and they cannot tweet about them either. They cannot send recruits unsolicited text messages or write unsolicited messages on Facebook walls.

Communication on both Facebook and Twitter are considered private, because on Facebook the recruit must accept the friend request and on Twitter the recruit must choose who to follow.

Direct messaging which can only be viewed by the two people involved (coach and recruit) on Twitter or Facebook is allowed. Any type of messaging, tweeting, etc, which can be viewed in the public domain, is not allowed.

"The main thing is, the recipient is in control of what they will and will not receive," said Matt Baysinger, the chair of the National Student-Athlete Advisory Council (SAAC). "There has been some frustration from coaches and athletic departments because we've gone against text messaging but have said okay to Facebook and Twitter. To us, it's because the prospective student-athlete is in control. No matter what the recruiting tool is, we want it to remain in control of the student-athlete."

Your child can set up a recruiting page on Facebook and Twitter. They can update these pages daily and also include video. Your child can research schools that they're interested in and find out if the coach has a Facebook or Twitter page, and choose to follow them.

Make sure to add your son or daughter's Facebook and Twitter URL to their resume ... and Mom, make sure their Facebook page is respectable. What they may think is acceptable may be totally different for us. Your adult eye can only help your child. Please be aware that many college coaches monitor the social media activities of prospective student-athletes. It doesn't matter if your child agrees with this or not. It happens.

Visit the NCAA website to learn more about current social media (electronic transmission) guidelines.

The most talented of athletes need to use social media to help network. YouTube can be used to highlight skills. The best thing here is that Facebook, Twitter and YouTube are all free to use. It just takes a little savvy and time, but can be well worth it.

"Using every available tool is necessary for a college recruit to maximize their recruiting potential."

How can your high school coach help?

Although the high school coach is not responsible for getting your son or daughter a college athletic scholarship, many college coaches will work directly with the high school coach to set up meetings and introductions.

NCSA asked former Division I recruiting coordinator Randy Taylor how college coaches can take advantage of the high school coach to further their recruiting efforts:

"A college coach would be making a huge mistake if they didn't work through the high school coach the whole way through the process. This allows the high school coach to feel as though they have some control and will help the college coach assure a good relationship for future recruits. Keep in mind, at some point in the future, the college coach will want to recruit a prospect from the same school, and the better the relationship, the more inclined a high school coach will be to grant access to his players. That access is crucial."

"Also, there are certain times when the college coach is unable to contact the recruit based on the recruiting timeline, so rather than contact the recruit directly and violate the rules, the college coach will express interest through the high school coach. With the accelerated pace of college recruiting, coaches are exploring every way to connect with a recruit as early as possible, and the high school coach happens to be one of those outlets. This might involve sending recruiting letters to the high school coach regarding one of their players, making a phone call to request an honest assessment, or even making an offer. The high school coach is really a key part of the relationship that the college coach needs to develop with a recruit."

HOW IMPORTANT IS SEPTEMBER FIRST TO THE HIGH SCHOOL STUDENT-ATHLETE?

September first is the turning-point for the high school student-athlete who wants to play at the next level. Please make a point to read *The Guide for College*

Bound Student Athletes published by the NCAA. This is a free publication found at ncaapublications.com.

For seniors

By September first of your child's senior year, the majority of Division I scholarship offers have already been issued and final evaluations are being completed.

Division II and III recruiting activity will begin to pick up. As a senior, the student-athlete should now evaluate where they stand. How many colleges have you visited with your son or daughter? How many college coaches have made contact with your child?

Specifically for football, September first marks the beginning of the evaluation period. The other sports will soon follow. By the end of September you should have begun looking at applications and school requirements. Help your child make a list of coaches that are interested in them and match them against their academic program offerings. They should also visit the school's athletic website to gain a greater understand of the school's sports program. If the school doesn't offer what they want, they should take it off their list and move on.

It is important to understand that Division II, III and NAIA coaches often wait until senior year before showing significant interest.

For juniors

For majority of sports, college coaches can begin to show serious interest. DI and DII coaches are allowed to send written recruiting information. Men's basketball and men's ice hockey have different dates. If your child emails a DI or DII coach, the coach may respond directly. Many student-athletes will begin receiving scholarship offers from colleges. Please make sure that your child responds back to all emails and letters, regardless of their level of interest.

Recruiting doesn't start on September first of your child's junior year … it actually starts sooner.

For freshmen and sophomores

If you know that your child wants to play at the next level … start now! A serious recruiting game plan, begun in these earlier years, will ultimately have more success than if they waited until their junior and senior years.

Here is what can be done as a freshman or sophomore. Note that if your child is a junior or senior and the following has not been done, they should get this list completed as soon as possible.

- Be evaluated. It is important that each student-athlete know what they need to improve, in order to reach their ideal level of play (Division I, II or III).
- Develop an athletic and academic resume.
- Start researching colleges.
- Start reaching out to college coaches through letters, phone calls and unofficial visits. If you are not sure how to do this, hiring an organization such as NCSA will be a great help.
- Both you and your child should be educated about the recruiting process. Start talking to recruiters now.

The work that you and your child do in freshman and sophomore years can have a positive affect on where they stand in their junior and senior years, because many college coaches start compiling their list of junior and sophomores. Some college coaches begin putting their recruiting lists together as early as the seventh and eight grades.

What official visits really mean

Before we talk about the "official" visit, let's take one more look at the "unofficial" visit. The unofficial visit is a great way for your child to meet coaches at college open houses, see what types of campus they like, and begin to make decisions. Or, even better, begin to rule out what they know they don't like!

Over an eight-month period, my son and I visited several colleges. Prior to our first visit we spent a lot of time on CollegeBoard.com and did some research. In looking for colleges we had a process that helped him narrow down his choices.

- Majors: Miles had three interests. We therefore targeted schools that offered at least two of the three.
- Cost: We had a budget for out-of-pocket expenses. Not necessarily for the cost of tuition.
- Distance: The school had to be within driving distance.
- Football – Next we narrowed the list down to

schools with all of the above and a football program. For us football was the last criterion because we wanted to make sure that he wanted to go to the school even if he didn't play football. As a parent, I understand that the cost of college can be high. However, sending your child to a school they don't like, just because they can play a sport may not be the best choice. If something happens and they can no longer play, then your child is left at a school where they won't be happy, or at a school that they love, but is not affordable.

• College visits were planned – At each visit he spoke with admissions and a football coach. At most of them he also got to meet with a professor from one of his areas of interest. We visited dorms and ate lunch on campus. The food was very important to him. We also looked at other activities offered by the school, such as clubs and intramural sports.

After each visit I asked Miles the same question: "If you don't play football here, would you still want to come here?" If he said "no," the school was removed from the list.

If you cover all of the above during your child's junior year, when their senior years comes around and official visits are offered, you and your child are prepared for this next important step.

What do you do if your son or daughter is invited for an official visit?

Go on the visit, but ask questions first. You need to know if you will be reimbursed for your expenses. If it's an overnight visit for your child, you want to know where and with whom they will be staying.

What does this mean?

It means that your son or daughter has made it to the next level in the recruiting process for that school. Congratulations!

How can you maximize this once in a lifetime opportunity for your son or daughter?

Approach it as you would a new job. If you didn't have the opportunity to visit the school beforehand, go online and read as much about it as possible. Help prepare your son or daughter for this adventure.

So what does the official visit really mean?

- Your son or daughter is being considered by the coach and are high on their list.
- The coaching staff is looking to see if your son or daughter is interested in their program.
- This is not an offer.

There are very specific NCAA rules regarding official visits, including having your son or daughter's official transcript on file before they arrive on campus. Make sure you understand these rules prior to taking your child on an official visit.

An official visit doesn't mean that your child will receive a scholarship or admission to that college.

Take pictures and lots of notes. Have your child make a list of everyone they meet, and send a thank-you note when they get home.

"LESSONS YOUR CHILD CAN *LIVE* WITH"

Lesson X — Don't forget to say thanks to those who have helped along the way

Every step through the process, your son or daughter should send a thank-you note.

If they've the opportunity to meet with admissions or a professor, as well as coaches a thank-you note should be sent.

ATHLETIC NATIONAL LETTER OF INTENT/SCHOLARSHIP OFFER

The ever-sought-after NLT! This is what every promising high school student-athlete is looking for who wants to play at the Division I and II levels. (Remember, there are no scholarships offered at the Division III level). Keep in mind, as we pointed out earlier, that only a very small fraction of the total number of student-athletes will receive this letter.

So what is this national letter of intent? First, it is an athletic scholarship for one year. It is a contract.

Please note that it doesn't necessarily guarantee admission to the college. The student-athlete must still meet the college academic requirements. The athletic scholarship doesn't guarantee a roster spot, and the scholarship can be lost due to bad grades, behavior, and violation of team rules.

If your child is fortunate enough to receive a national letter of intent, sit with them and read it carefully. It will detail what they can and cannot do, and it will define the amount of the scholarship. If it isn't a full scholarship, you will still need to determine if you cannot afford the balance of the tuition and expenses, such as room and board, books and meal plan. Although Division III may not give athletic scholarships, they may have other monies available for your child. So that in the end, the out-of-pocket may be less at a Division III school... not always, but worth looking into.

One last note, Mom, you too are being recruited. The college coaches are looking at you as well as your son or daughter. They're watching how you interact with your son or whether or not you allow your daughter to answer questions for herself. Remember they not only get our children, they get us too for the next four years. This is one of the things I learned from NCSA.

NCSA evaluates each recruit and makes sure that they're matched according to their playing level. Having gone through the process with NCSA as a parent, I know that I would not have known half of what I learned if it were not for the weekly emails we received and numerous videos that they produce.

Obviously, you are serious about your child's high school sports career, and if you are just as serious about your child's possibility of playing at the next level, a professional recruiter is worth the time to look into.

Finally, we send our children to college to get an education, not to play sports.

Four years after high school,
after the last college game
of the season is played,
and all the glory fades from the wins past,
it is our educated college graduates
who are the winners!

17 – A MOM'S "TWO CENTS"

A mother's words are some of the most important to our children. Take a moment to offer your "two cents" and then share them with your high school student-athlete. This may help them to better understand why you do what you do.

Dear _____,

Although I love that you are involved in high school sports, I just want you to know that ...

_____

_____

_____

_____

_____

_____

_____

_____

_____

_____

_____

_____

_____

_____

_____

_____

_____

_____

_____

_____

_____

_____

_____

(If you have more than one child, make copies of this page)

Love, Mom

18 - Do's and Don'ts
FOR THE SPORT PARENT
By Michael A. Taylor

For Yourself – Do

- Get vicarious pleasure form your children's participation, but don't become overly ego-involved.
- Try to enjoy yourself at competitions. Your unhappiness can cause your child to feel guilty.
- Look relaxed, calm and positive and energized when watching your child compete. Your attitude influences how your child feels and performs.
- Have a life of your own outside of your child's sports participation.

For Other Parents - Do

- Make friends with other parents at events. Socializing can make the event more fun for you.
- Volunteer as much as you can. Youth sports depend upon the time and energy of involved parents.
- Police your own ranks: Work with other parents to ensure that all parents behave appropriately at practices and competitions.

For the Coach – Do

- Leave the coaching to the coaches.
- Give them any support they need to help them do their jobs better.
- Communicate with them about your child. You can learn about your child from each other.
- Inform them of relevant issues at home that might affect your child at practice.
- Inquire about the progress of your children. You have a right to know.
- Make the coaches your allies.

For Your Children – Do

- Provide guidance for your children, but don't force or pressure them.
- Assist them in setting realistic goals for participation.
- Emphasize fun, skill development and other benefits of sports participation, e.g., cooperation, competition, self-discipline, commitment.
- Show interest in their participation: help them get to practice, attend competitions, and ask questions.
- Provide a health perspective to help children understand success and failure.
- Emphasize and reward effort rather than results.
- Intervene if your child's behavior in unacceptable during practice or competitions.
- Understand that your child may need a break from sports occasionally.
- Give your child some space when needed. Part of sports participation involves them figuring things out for themselves.
- Keep a sense of humor. If you are having fun and laughing, so will your child.

- Provide regular encouragement.
- Be a healthy role model for your child by being positive and relaxed at competitions and by having balance in your life.
- Give them unconditional love: show them you love them whether they win or lose!

For Yourself – Don't Do

- Base your self-esteem and ego on the success of your child's sports participation.
- Care too much about how your child performs.
- Lose perspective about the importance of your child's sports participation.

With Other Parents – Don't Do

- Make enemies of other parents.
- Talk about others in the sports community. Talk to them. It is more constructive.

With the Coach – Don't Do

- Interfere with their coaching during practice or competitions.
- Work at cross-purposes with them. Make sure

you agree philosophically and practically on why your child is playing sports and what they may get out of sports.

With Your Children – Don't Do

- Expect your children to get anything more from their sport than a good time, physical fitness, mastery and love of a lifetime sport, and transferable life skills.
- Ignore your child's bad behavior in practice and competition.
- Ask the child to talk with you immediately after a competition.
- Show negative emotions while watching them perform.
- Make your child feel guilty for the time, energy and money you are spending and the sacrifices you are making.
- Think of your child's sports participation as an investment for which you expect a return.
- Live out your own dreams through your child's sports participation.
- Compare your child's progress with that of other children.

- Badger, harass, use sarcasm, threaten or use fear to motivate your child. It only demeans them and causes them to hate you.
- Expect anything from your child except their best effort.
- Ever do anything that will cause them to think less of themselves or of you!

You can help your child become a strong competitor by...

- Emphasizing and rewarding effort rather than outcome.
- Understanding that your child may need a break from sports occasionally.
- Encouraging and guiding your child, not forcing or pressuring them to compete.
- Emphasizing the importance of learning and transferring life skills such as hard work, self-discipline, teamwork, and commitment.
- Emphasizing the importance of having fun, learning new skills, and developing skills.
- Showing interest in their participation in sports, asking questions.
- Giving your child some space when needed.

Allow children to figure things out for themselves.

- Keeping a sense of humor. If you are having fun, so will your child.
- Giving unconditional love and support to your child, regardless of the outcome of the day's competition.
- Enjoying yourself at competitions. Make friends with other parents, socialize, and have fun.
- Looking relaxed, calm, and positive when watching your child compete.
- Realizing that your attitude and behaviors influences your child's performance.
- Having a balanced life of your own outside sports.

Don't...

- Think of your child's sport participation as an investment for which you want a return.
- Live out your dreams through your child.
- Do anything that will cause your child to be embarrassed.
- Feel that you need to motivate your child. This is the child's and coach's responsibility.

- Ignore your child's behavior when it is inappropriate. (Deal with it constructively so that it doesn't happen again.)
- Compare your child's performance to that of other children.
- Show negative emotions while you are watching your child at a competition.
- Expect your child to talk with you when they're upset.
- Base your self-esteem on the success of your child's sport participation.
- Care too much about how your child performs.
- Make enemies with other children's parents or the coach.
- Interfere, in any way, with coaching during competition or practice.
- Try to coach your child. Leave this to the coach.

Stress Relievers for Parents with Children in Sports

- Laugh. Go to a funny movie or do something silly with a friend.
- Take a 10-minute break and walk around the block.
- Light a candle and take a bubble bath in the

dark.

- Do nothing ... and don't feel guilty about it.
- Pay off your credit cards.
- Turn off the TV.
- Read a book or magazine.
- Read a classic book as a family.
- Make time for a hobby or activity you really love.
- Meet a good friend for coffee.
- Write your child's coach a note of thanks..
- Smile at someone.
- Sit outside on a warm summer night and watch the stars come out.
- Concede that you don't have to be proven right every time.
- As a family get involved with a project that helps someone less fortunate.
- Set up a carpool schedule for your kids' activities so you don't spend your life in the car.
- Set aside a day with no outside activities scheduled.
- Go to the church or synagogue of your choice.
- Schedule a meeting with your child's coach to discuss her (his) progress and establish agreed-upon goals.

• Avoid initiating or participating in the gym
gossip.

About Michael A. Taylor
Michael A. Taylor is a USGA Kinder Accreditation for Teachers (KAT & MELPD)
Instructor, serves on the USA Gymnastics Preschool Advisory Panel, is a UGA
Gymnastics National Safety Instructor, serves on the USA Gymnastics Safety
Review Board, and is a UGSA PDP I Video Clinic Administrator, an American Red
Cross CPR? First Aid and Sport Safety Instructor, and an American Sport
Education Program Coaching Principles (PDP II) Instructor. Michael is a Certified
National Youth Sports Administrator; an Instructor for the Standard University
based Positive Coaching Alliance, a long-time member of the United States Elite
Coaches Association and a former gym owner.

GOD BLESS
all of us
who have the
good fortune
to be parents of a
high school
student-athlete!

Books To Read

Athletes Wanted: Learn the tools for maximizing athletic scholarship and life potential
By Chris Krause, founder of The National Collegiate Scouting Association
Published by Collegiate Athletic Educational Foundation
Provide by Quality Bokks Inc (May 1, 2009)

Mom 3.0: Marketing WITH Today's Mothers by Leveraging New Media & Technology
By Maria Bailey T. Bailey
Published by Wyatt-MacKenzie Publishing (September 24, 2008)

World's Toughest Job
By Annette Clifford
Published by Annette Clifford (2009)

101 Ways to Be a Terrific Sports Parent: Making Athletics a Positive Experience for Your Child
By Joel Fish, Susan Magee
Published by Fireside; Original edition (September 2, 2003)

The High school Sports Parent: Developing Triple-Impact Competitors
By Jim Thompson
Published by Balance Sports Publishing (August 1, 2009)

Staying Connected to Your Child: How to Keep Them Talking to You and How to Hear What They're Really Saying
By Michael Riera
Published by Da Capo Press (April 15, 2003)

A Fine Young Man: What Parents, Mentors, and Educators Can Do to Shape Adolescent Boys into Exceptional Men
By Michael Gurian
Published by Tarcher; 1st Trade Pbk. Ed edition (April 1, 1999)

Energy to Burn: The Ultimate Food and Nutrition Guide to Fuel Your Active Life
By Julie Upton and Jenna Bell-Wilson
Published by Wiley; 1 edition (March 23, 2009)

Get Out of My Life, but First Could You Drive Me & Cheryl to the Mall: A Parent's Guide to the New Teenager, Revised and Updated
By Anthony E. Wolf Ph.D.
Published by Farrar, Straus and Giroux; Revised edition (August 1, 2002)

Nancy Clark's Sports Nutrition Guidebook
By Nancy Clark, MS, RD
Published by Human Kinetics; 4 edition (March 14, 2008)

Whose Game Is It, Anyway?: A Guide to Helping Your Child Get the Most from Sports, Organized by Age and Stage
By Richard D. Ginsburg,, Stephen Durant, Amy Baltzell
Published by Mariner Books (March 10, 2006)

WEBSITES AND BLOGS

thehighschoolsportsmom.blogspot.com
Blog with Michelle Winfrey
The High School Sports Mom

PHSEDGroup.com
Parents High School Sports Education Group

twitter.com/MichelleWinfrey
Follow Michelle Winfrey on Twitter

My Child Plays High School Sports – Facebook Fan Page
Share your thoughts, concerns and experiences with high
school sports. A great place to network with other parents of
high school student-athletes.

ncsasports.org
National Collegiate Scouting Association
Blog with NCSA at http://blog.ncsasports.org

Follow NCSA on Twitter at twitter.com/ncsa

ncaa.org
National Collegiate Athletic Association

eligibilitycenter.org
NCAA Eligibility Center

ncaa.com
The official online store for NCAA sports

nfhs.org
About the National Federation of State High School
Associations (NFHS)

nationalunderclassmen.com
Schuman's National Underclassmen Combine
The Premier Underclass Combine & Showcase.

Blog with David Schuman, CEO, National Underclassmen
Combines at
nucfootball.blogspot.com

Following NUC on Twitter at
twitter.com/NUCFootball

TAKKLE.com

The TAKKLE Squad
The Ultimate High School Sports Blog
Blog with TAKKLE at blog.takkle.com

beRecruited.com
Blog with beRecruited at blogs.bRecruited.com

highschoolsports.net

stack.com
For the athlete, by the athlete

usasf.net/safety/cheerrules
US All-Star Federation

sportsconcussion.com

rivals.com

Sports and Nutrition the Winning Connection (University of Illinois Connection)
urbanext.illinois.edu/hsnut/hsath3b.html

nucfootball.com

msgvarsity.com

MomsTeam.com
The trusted source for youth sport parents

On your mark, get set – GO!